ANALYSIS OF
SHAOLIN
CHIN NA

BY DR. YANG JWING-MING

YMAA Publication Center
4354 Washington Street
Boston, Massachusetts, 02131

ISBN:0-940871-04-1

15

Publisher's Cataloging in Publication
(Prepared by Quality Books Inc.)

Yang, Jwing-Ming, 1946-
    Analysis of Shaolin chin na : instructor's manual for all martial
styles / Yang Jwing-Ming.
        p. cm.
        ISBN: 0-940871-15-7 (hardcover)
        ISBN: 0-940871-04-1 (pbk.)

    1. Martial arts. I. Title. II. Title: Shaolin chin na

GV1112   796.8
                                                    QBI90-318

Disclaimer:
The author and publisher of this material are NOT RESPONSIBLE in any
manner whatsoever for any injury which may occur through reading or following the instructions in this manual.
The activities, physical or otherwise, described in this material may be too
strenuous or dangerous for some people, and the reader(s) should consult a
physician before engaging in them.

Printed in Canada.

To My White Crane Grandmaster Gin Shao-Fon

ACKNOWLEDGEMENTS

Thanks to A. Reza Farman-Farmaian for the photography, Rami Rones for general help, Eric Hoffman and James O'Leary, Jr. for proofing the manuscript and for contributing many valuable suggestions and discussions, and Christer Manning for the drawings and cover design. Special thanks to Alan Dougall for his editing.

ABOUT THE AUTHOR
DR. YANG JWING-MING

Dr. Yang Jwing-Ming was born in Taiwan, Republic of China, in 1946. He started his Wushu (Kung Fu) training at the age of fifteen under the Shaolin White Crane (Pai Huo) Master Cheng Gin-Gsao. In thirteen years of study (1961-1974) under Master Cheng, Dr. Yang became an expert in White Crane defense and attack, which includes both the use of barehands and of various weapons such as saber, staff, spear, trident, and two short rods. With the same master he also studied White Crane Chin Na, massage, and herbal treatment. At the age of sixteen Dr. Yang began the study of Tai Chi Chuan (Yang Style) under Master Kao Tao. After learning from Master Kao, Dr. Yang continued his study and research of Tai Chi Chuan with several masters in Taipei. In Taipei he became qualified to teach Tai Chi. He has mastered the Tai Chi barehand sequence, pushing hands, the two-man fighting sequence, Tai Chi sword, Tai Chi saber, and internal power development.

When Dr. Yang was eighteen years old he entered Tamkang College in Taipei Hsien to study Physics. In college, he began the study of traditional Shaolin Long Fist (Chang Chuan) with Master Li Mao-Ching at the Tamkang College Kuoshu Club (1964-1968), and eventually became an assistant instructor under Master Li. In 1971 he completed his M.S. degree in Physics at the National Taiwan University, and then served in the Chinese Air Force from 1971-1972. In the service, Dr. Yang taught Physics at the Junior Academy of the Chinese Air Force while also teaching Wushu. After being honorably discharged in 1972, he returned to Tamkang College to teach Physics and resume study under Master Li Mao-Ching. From Master Li, Dr. Yang learned Northern style Wushu, which includes both barehand (especially kicking) techniques and numerous weapons.

In 1974, Dr. Yang came to the United States to study Mechanical Engineering at Purdue University. At the request of a few students, Dr. Yang began to teach Kung Fu which resulted in the foundation of the Purdue University Chinese Kung Fu Research Club in the spring of 1975. While at Purdue, Dr. Yang also taught college-credited courses in Tai Chi Chuan. In May of 1978, he was awarded a Ph.D. in Mechanical Engineering by Purdue.

Currently, Dr. Yang and his family reside in Massachusetts. In January of 1984, he gave up his engineering career to devote more time to research, writing, and teaching at Yang's Martial Arts Association (YMAA) in Boston.

In summary, Dr. Yang has been involved in Chinese Wushu (Kung Fu) for more than twenty years. During this time, he has spent thirteen years learning Shaolin White Crane (Pai Huo), Shaolin Long Fist (Chang Chuan), and Tai Chi Chuan. Dr. Yang has eighteen years of instructional experience: seven years in Taiwan, five years at Purdue University, two years in Houston, Texas, and four years in Boston, Massachusetts.

Dr. Yang has published eight other volumes on the martial arts:

1. *Shaolin Chin Na;* Unique Publications, Inc., 1980.

2. *Shaolin Long Fist Kung Fu;* Unique Publications, Inc., 1981.
3. *Yang Style Tai Chi Chuan;* Unique Publications, Inc., 1981.
4. *Introduction to Ancient Chinese Weapons;* Unique Publications, Inc., 1985.
5. *Chi Kung - Health and Martial Arts;* Yang's Martial Arts Association (YMAA), 1985.
6. *Northern Shaolin Sword;* Yang's Martial Arts Association (YMAA), 1985.
7. *Advanced Yang Style Tai Chi Chuan, Vol. 1, Tai Chi Theory and Tai Chi Jings;* Yang's Martial Arts Association (YMAA), 1986.
8. *Advanced Yang Style Tai Chi Chuan, Vol. 2, Martial Applications;* Yang's Martial Arts Association (YMAA), 1986.

Dr. Yang plans to publish a number of additional books including:

1. *Shii Soei Chi Kung*
2. *Chi Kung and Health*
3. *Chi Kung and Martial Arts*
4. *Southern White Crane Kung Fu*
5. *Northern Shaolin Staff*
6. *Northern Shaolin Saber*
7. *Northern Shaolin Spear*

Dr. Yang has also published the following videotapes:

1. *Yang Style Tai Chi Chuan and Its Applications,* Yang's Martial Arts Association (YMAA), 1984.
2. *Shaolin Long Fist Kung Fu - Lien Bu Chuan and Its Applications,* Yang's Martial Arts Association (YMAA), 1985.
3. *Shaolin Long Fist Kung Fu - Gung Li Chuan and Its Applications,* Yang's Martial Arts Association (YMAA), 1986.
4. *Shaolin Chin Na,* Yang's Martial Arts Association (YMAA), 1987.

Several videotapes have also been scheduled for publication:

1. *Chi Kung*
2. *Shaolin Long Fist Kung Fu - Yi Lu Mei Fu*
3. *Shaolin Long Fist Kung Fu - Shaw Fu Ien*
4. *Shaolin Long Fist Kung Fu - Shih Tzu Tan*
5. *Tai Chi Martial Applications and Pushing Hands*
6. *Tai Chi Fighting Set and Its Applications*
7. *Yang Style Tai Chi Sword and Its Applications*

Dr. Yang Jwing-Ming

FOREWORD

Since I came to the United States in 1974 I have had a dream that, in addition to obtaining my Ph.D., I could help to popularize the traditional Chinese martial arts in this country. From Purdue University Chinese Kung Fu Club, to Yang's Shaolin Kung Fu Academy (Houston), to Yang's Martial Arts Academy (YMAA), and now Yang's Martial Arts Association (YMAA) in Boston, my dream has gradually become reality. Now that I have purchased property in the Jamaica Plain area of Boston, YMAA finally has a stable headquarters from which to carry out the work.

In the seven years since 1980 I have completed nine volumes on the Chinese martial arts, and plan to publish ten more in the next ten years. YMAA has also started publishing videotapes, with two to four tapes scheduled to be published every year for the next ten years. I hope YMAA will become a research and study center for high quality martial arts books and tapes. Branch schools will be opened in the next few years, and once we can build a new building next to the present one, we will have room for related activities such as an acupuncture center, a Chi Kung training center, Chinese herb center, Chinese massage center, and a bookstore and library in addition to the now existing publication center and Tai Chi and Shaolin training centers. The newly purchased building on 8000 square feet of property is the first step to fulfilling my dream.

I am indebted to so many enthusiastic students who have sacrificed their time and money over the past eleven years to help me build this school from nothing. I feel certain that people will continue to offer their help to speed the growth of YMAA. I am deeply touched by all the help that so many have offered, and I will not hesitate to share my knowledge with my students and with all sincere and humble martial artist in this country.

I hope in the future to incorporate YMAA and to sell stock to the members. If this dream comes true we will be able to build a three story building at the headquarters location.

Finally, I want to express my deepest respect and thanks to those masters who have contributed so much effort to the growth and popularization of the Chinese martial arts.

PREFACE

Chin Na has been a part of Chinese martial arts since their very beginning. Chin Na covers a wide scale of defensive and offensive techniques from the very fundamental to the very advanced. The fundamental techniques can be learned by any martial artist or even by someone without any martial arts experience. These fundamental techniques can easily be adapted and incorporated into any martial style such as Judo, Wrestling, Karate, or Tae Kwon Do to increase the range of responses. Once a person has mastered all these fundamental techniques, he can continue his study in the advanced Chin Na, which is so deep that it will take more than 20 years to learn, practice, and master. It is knowledge without end or limit. When Chin Na reaches an advanced level, the application of Chi (internal energy) and Jing becomes very difficult to understand. Without oral instruction from a qualified master, it is almost impossible to learn and master. When you have reached this level, you have reached the level which is beyond what a book can describe. It is learned from sensing, feeling, and inspiration.

Since the author published his first martial book *Shaolin Chin Na* in 1980, many martial artists in both Chinese Kung Fu as well as other styles have read it, researched the techniques, and practiced them. A number of martial schools have used it as a textbook for grappling training.

A great number of readers have written or phoned. The author has noted that there are a few questions which arise again and again. The most common questions are: Which techniques can be used to counterattack or to prevent the opponent from controlling me? Which muscle or joint do specific techniques use for control, and what are the principles of the control? What is the anatomical structure of the area being controlled, and what damage will occur if more pressure is applied? How do I take care of injuries? How does Chin Na differ from Jujitsu and Aikido?

Many people who try to learn techniques from the book encounter certain common difficulties. Often people do not catch the key point of each technique, and so the techniques seem to be ineffective. If the technique is done incorrectly or the stance is wrong, the opponent can easily escape or counterattack.

The first Chin Na book was only an introductory text, and covered only the surface level of principles and techniques. It has served its purpose of helping people to start Chin Na training, but it was not designed to answer all possible questions or to give all the details of individual techniques.

This second book has been written to build upon the foundation which the first book has laid. Rather than repeat basic theory and descriptions, this book will discuss more deeply the techniques of dividing the muscle/tendon (Fen Gin), misplacing the bone (Tsuoh Guu), sealing the breath (Bih Chi), sealing the vein (Duann Mie), and grabbing the muscle/tendon (Jua Gin). However, advanced cavity press (Tien Hsueh) or meridian press (Dim Mak) will not be discussed in depth. The principles and deeper theory of this technique would require a whole volume for a balanced discussion. It is difficult to learn cavity press techniques just from a book, and without a qualified master's oral instruction, it is also extremely dangerous for both yourself and your partners.

This book is designed primarily for instructors who are teaching Chin Na techniques, though any martial artist with some Chin Na experience will also find it useful. Beginners to Chin Na should read the author's first Chin Na book: *Shaolin Chin Na* and use this volume as a reference book.

This book will first briefly review basic Chin Na principles, and show the fundamental training. This constitutes the foundation of the Chin Na techniques. It will then present about 150 fundamental Chin Na techniques and some of their counterattacks, in separate chapters on fingers, wrists, arms, and so on. Finally, Chapter 11 will discuss the treatment of common injuries which might occur during Chin Na practice.

TABLE OF CONTENTS

CHAPTER 1
GENERAL INTRODUCTION

1-1. Introduction

"Chin" in Chinese means "to seize or catch", in the way an eagle seizes a rabbit or a policeman catches a murderer (Chin Shiong). "Na" means "to hold and control". Therefore, Chin Na can be translated as "seize and control". In addition to the grabbing techniques implied by the name, the art of Chin Na also includes techniques which utilize pressing and even striking. Generally speaking, grabbing Chin Na is more fundamental, while pressing and striking techniques are more advanced. Grabbing Chin Na techniques control and lock the opponent's joints or muscles/tendons so he cannot move, thus neutralizing his fighting ability. Pressing Chin Na techniques are used to numb the opponent's limbs, to cause him to lose consciousness, or even to kill him. Pressing Chin Na is usually applied to the Chi cavities to affect the Chi circulation to the organs or the brain. Pressing techniques are also frequently used on nerve endings to cause extreme pain and unconsciousness. Chin Na striking techniques are applied to vital points, and can be very deadly. Cavities on the Chi channels can be attacked, or certain vital areas struck to rupture arteries. All of these techniques serve to "seize and control" the opponent.

Chin Na techniques can be generally categorized as:

1. "Fen Gin" (dividing the muscle/tendon)
2. "Tsuoh Guu" (misplacing the bone)
3. "Bih Chi" (sealing the breath)
4. "Duann Mie" (sealing or blocking the vein/artery) or "Dim Mak" (vein/artery press)
5. "Tien Hsueh" (cavity press) or "Dim Mak" (meridian press)

Within these categories, Fen Gin also includes "Jua Gin" (grabbing muscle/tendon) and Tien Hsueh also includes "Na Hsueh" (grabbing or pressing cavities).

Generally, dividing the muscle/tendon, misplacing the bone, and some techniques of sealing the breath are relatively easy to learn and the theory behind them is easy to understand. They usually require only muscular strength and practice to make the control effective. When these same techniques are used to break bones or injure joints or tendons, you usually need to use Jing. (For a discussion of Jing, see the author's book *Advanced Yang Style Tai Chi Chuan, Vol. 1, Tai Chi Theory and Tai Chi Jing*). Sealing the vein/artery and pressing the cavities requires detailed knowledge of the location, depth, and timing of the cavities, development of Yi, Chi, and Jing, and special hand forms and techniques. This usually requires oral instruction by a qualified master, not only because the knowledge is deep, but also because most of the techniques are learned from sensing and feeling. Many of the techniques can easily cause death. For this reason a master will normally only pass this knowledge down to students who are moral and trustworthy.

Nobody can tell exactly when Chin Na was first used. It probably began the first time one man grabbed another with the intention of controlling him. Grabbing the opponent's limbs or weapon is one of the most basic and instinctive ways to immobilize the opponent or control his actions.

Because of their practicality, Chin Na techniques have been trained right along with other fighting techniques since the beginning of Chinese martial arts many thousands of years ago. Although no system has sprung up which practices only Chin Na, almost every martial style has Chin Na mixed in with its other techniques. Even in Japan, Korea, and other oriental countries which have been significantly affected by Chinese culture, the indigenous martial styles have Chin Na techniques mixed in to a greater or lesser degree.

Generally speaking, since martial styles in southern China specialize in hand techniques and close range fighting, they tend to have better developed Chin Na techniques, and they tend to rely more upon them than the northern styles do. Because southern martial styles emphasize hand conditioning more than the northern styles, they tend to use more muscles for grabbing and cavity press. In addition, because of the emphasis on short range fighting, southern styles emphasize sticking and adhering more, and techniques are usually applied with a circular motion which can set the opponent up for a Chin Na control without his feeling the preparation. Footwork is also considered a very important part of the training for a southern martial artist. Remember that these statements are only generalities, and there are northern styles which also emphasize these things.

In Chinese internal styles such as Tai Chi and Liu Ho Ba Fa, neutralization is usually done with a circular motion, and so the Chin Na techniques tend to be smooth and round. Often the opponent will be controlled before he realizes that a technique is being applied. In coordination with circular stepping, circular Chin Na can be used to pull the opponent's root and throw him away.

Japanese and Korean Jujitsu and Aikido are based on the same principles as Chin Na. Since these countries were significantly influenced by Chinese culture, it seems probable that Chinese Chin Na also influenced their indigenous martial arts.

Since fundamental Chin Na techniques can be used to seize and control a criminal without injuring or killing him, they have been an important part of the training for constables, government officers, and today's policemen. Around 527 A.D. the Shaolin temple became involved in the martial arts. Since many non-lethal Chin Na techniques are very effective, the martial artists at the temple extensively researched, developed, and trained them. In the late Ching dynasty in the 19th century, Shaolin techniques were taught to people in the general population, and Chin Na techniques were passed down along with the different martial styles which were developed in the Shaolin temple.

Many Chin Na techniques were also developed for use with weapons specially designed to seize the opponent's weapon. If your opponent is disarmed, he is automatically in a disadvantageous situation. For example, the hook of the hook sword or the hand guard of a Sai were designed for this purpose. In this volume we will discuss only barehand Chin Na techniques. Weapon Chin Na will be discussed in future volumes on specific weapons.

1-2. General Principles of Chin Na

Although Chin Na techniques from one Kung Fu style may seem quite different from the techniques of another style, the theories and principles of application remain the same. These theories and principles form the root of all the Chin Na techniques. If you adhere to these roots, your Chin Na will continue to grow and improve, but if you ignore these roots, your Chin Na will always remain undeveloped. In this section we will discuss these general theories and principles.

Before we discuss each Chin Na category, you should understand that there is no technique which is perfect for all situations. What you do depends upon what your opponent does, and since your opponent will not stand still and just let you control him, you must be able to adapt your Chin Na to fit the circumstances. Like all other martial techniques, your Chin Na must respond to and follow the situation, and so it needs to be skillful, alive, fast, and powerful. You should furthermore understand that Chin Na must be done by surprise. In grabbing Chin Na you have to grasp your opponent's body, and so if your opponent is aware of your intention it will be extremely difficult for you to successfully apply the technique. In such a case you may be obliged to use a cavity strike Chin Na instead of a grabbing technique.

It is usually much easier to strike the opponent than to control him. Subduing an opponent through a Chin Na controlling technique is a way to show mercy to someone you do not want to injure. To successfully apply a grabbing Chin Na you often need to fake or strike the opponent first to set him up for your controlling technique. For example, you can use a punch to cause your opponent to block, and when he blocks, you quickly grab his hand and use Chin Na to control him. Alternatively, you might kick his shin first to draw his attention to his leg, and immediately grab his hand and control him.

As mentioned, there are five categories of Chin Na: 1. Fen Gin or Jua Gin (dividing the muscle/tendon or grabbing the muscle/tendon). 2. Tsuoh Guu (misplacing the bone). 3. Bih Chi (sealing the breath). 4. Dim Mak or Duann Mie (vein/artery press or sealing the vein/artery). 5. Dim Mak or Tien Hsueh (meridian press or cavity press). This book will discuss all of these categories in detail except the last one, which will be discussed only on an introductory level, because it requires an in-depth understanding of Chi circulation, acupuncture, and specialized training techniques.

One additional point needs to be mentioned here, and that is that very often Chin Na techniques make use of principles from several categories at once. For example, many techniques simultaneously use the principles of dividing the muscle/tendon and misplacing the bone.

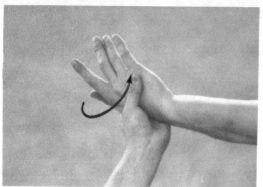

Figure 1-1.

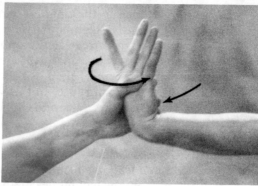

Figure 1-2.

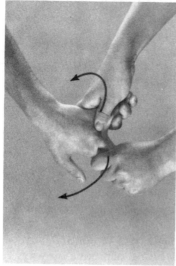

Figure 1-3.

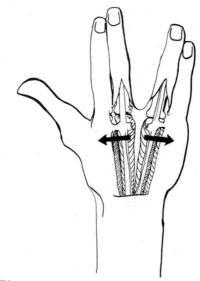

Figure 1-4.

1. Fen Gin or Jua Gin (dividing the muscle/tendon or grabbing the muscle/tendon): 分筋 抓筋

Fen in Chinese means to divide, Jua means to grab and Gin means tendon, sinew, or muscle. Fen Gin or Jua Gin Chin Na refer to techniques which tear apart the opponent's muscles or tendons, or even detach the tendons from the bones. Muscles contain nerves and many Chi branch channels, so when you tear a muscle or tendon, not only do you cause sensations of pain to travel to the brain, you also directly or indirectly affect the Chi and interfere with the normal functioning of the organs. If the pain is great enough it can disturb the Chi and seriously damage the organs, and in extreme cases even cause death. For this reason, when you are in extreme pain your brain may give the order for you to pass out. Once you are unconscious, the Chi circulation will significantly decrease, which will limit damage to the organs and perhaps save your life.

Fen Gin Chin Na uses two main ways to divide the muscle/tendon. One way is to twist the opponent's joint and then bend. Twisting the joint also twists the muscles/tendons (Figure 1-1). If you bend the joint at the same time, you can tear the tendons off the bone (Figure 1-2). The other method is to split and tear the muscle/tendon apart without twisting. The most common place to do this is the fingers (Figures 1-3 and 1-4).

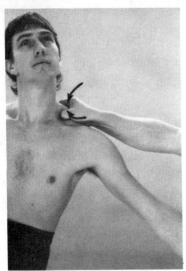

Figure 1-5.

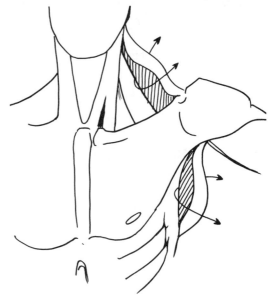

Figure 1-6.

Jua Gin (grabbing the muscle/tendon) relies upon the strength of the fingers to grab, press, and then pull the opponent's large muscles or tendons. This causes pain by overextending the muscles and tendons. The shoulder muscles/tendons are a common target (Figures 1-5 and 1-6). Jua Gin Chin Na is used particularly by the Eagle Claw and Tiger Claw styles. Although Jua Gin is usually classified with Fen Gin Chin Na, many Chinese martial artists separate the two categories because the principle used to divide the muscle/tendon is different.

2. Tsuoh Guu (misplacing the bone): 錯骨

Tsuoh means wrong, disorder, or to place wrongly, and Guu means bone. Tsuoh Guu therefore are Chin Na techniques which put bones in the wrong positions. These techniques are usually applied to the joints. If you examine the structure of a joint, you will see that the bones are connected to each other by ligaments and cartilage, and that the muscles around and over the joints are connected to the bones by tendons (Figure 1-7). When a joint is bent backward (Figure 1-8) or twisted and bent in the wrong direction (Figure 1-9), it can cause extreme pain, the ligament can be torn off the bone, and the bones can be pulled apart. Strictly speaking, it is very difficult to use dividing the muscle/tendon and misplacing the bone techniques separately. When one is used, generally the other one is also more or less simultaneously applied.

3. Bih Chi (sealing the breath): 閉氣

Bih in Chinese means to close, seal, or shut, and Chi (more specifically Korn Chi) means air. Bih Chi is the technique of preventing the opponent from inhaling, thereby causing him to pass out. There are three categories of Bih Chi, differing in the approach to sealing.

The first category is the direct sealing of the windpipe. You can grab your opponent's throat with your fingers, or compress his throat with your arm, and prevent him from inhaling. Alternatively, you can use your fingers to press or strike the base of his throat (Figure 1-10) to stop him from inhaling. Attacking this area causes the muscles around the windpipe to contract and close the windpipe.

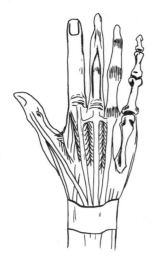

Figure 1-7.

Figure 1-8.

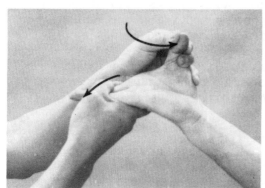

Figure 1-9.

Figure 1-10.

The second category of Bih Chi is striking the muscles which surround the lungs. Because of the protection which the ribs afford, it is very difficult to strike the muscles around the lungs directly. However, some of these muscles extend beyond the ribs. When they are attacked, they contract in pain and compress the lungs, preventing inhalation. Two muscle groups in the stomach are commonly used this way (Figure 1-11).

Finally, the last category of sealing the breath is cavity press or nerve ending strike. The principle of this category is very similar to that of the muscle strikes, the only difference being that cavities are struck rather than muscle groups. This category is normally much more difficult both in principle and technique. However, when it is done correctly it is more effective than striking the muscles.

If you take a look at the structure of the chest area, you will see that the lungs are well protected by the ribs, which prevent outside forces from damaging the lungs and other organs. You will notice also that each rib is

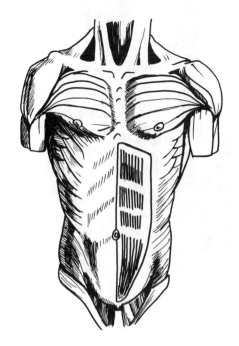 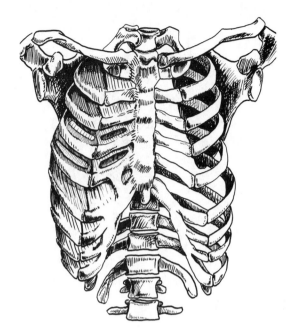

Figure 1-11.   Figure 1-12.

not a single piece of bone wrapping around your body, but rather two pieces of bone, connected by strong ligaments and cartilage (Figure 1-12). When an outside force strikes the chest, the ribs act like a spring or an elastic ball to bounce the attacking force away or bounce yourself backward in order to protect the lungs and heart. This construction makes it very hard to cause the lungs to compress by striking the chest. You should also understand that the muscles which are outside the ribs will not compress the lungs when they contract, because the ribs will protect the lungs. Therefore, in order to cause contraction of the lungs you must strike particular acupuncture cavities or the ends of the nerves which emerge from the lung area underneath the ribs (Figure 1-13). Striking these cavities accurately and to the right depth will affect the Chi in the muscles around the lungs, causing them to contract. Alternatively, you can strike the nerve endings. This causes pain to penetrate the ribs and shock the internal muscles surrounding the lungs into contraction, thus sealing the breath.

4. Dim Mak or Duann Mie (vein/artery press or sealing the vein/artery): 點脉 斷脉

Dim Mak is also known as Tien Mie, which is simply the same words spoken in a different dialect. Tien in Chinese means to point or press with a finger. Mie means Chi channels or meridians (Chi Mie), or blood vessels (Shiee Mie). Therefore, Tien Mie means to strike or press either the Chi meridians or the veins/arteries. When it means to strike or press the vein/artery, it is also called Duann Mie (sealing the vein/artery). Duann means to break, seal, or stop. Sometimes it is also called Tien Shiee (blood press), such as when the artery in the temple is struck and ruptured. When Dim Mak means to strike or press the cavities on the Chi channels, it is also called Tien Hsueh (cavity press). Here, we will discuss Duann Mie and leave the discussion of Tien Hsueh for later.

In principle, Duann Mie can be done either by striking or pressing. A striking Duann Mie Chin Na can rupture the blood vessel and stop the

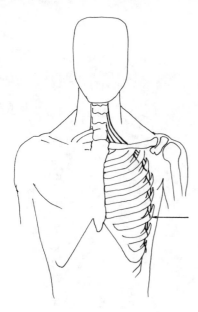

Figure 1-13.

Figure 1-14.

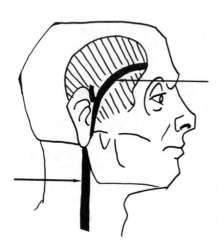

Figure 1-15.

Figure 1-16.

blood circulation, which usually causes death. For example, when the temple is struck, the muscles in that area will tighten up and rupture the artery (Figures 1-14 and 1-15). A pressing Duann Mie Chin Na can also stop or seal the blood circulation. For example, sealing the neck artery will stop the blood circulation to your head and thus cut down the oxygen supply to the brain. This will cause unconsciousness or even death. There are two major arteries, one on either side of your neck, which supply oxygen to your brain (Figures 1-15 and 1-16). When either or both of these are struck or pressed, the flow of blood to the brain can be stopped. Sometimes the muscles on the side of the neck remain tensed. If you do not know how to revive the victim, he will die from the lack of oxygen. Therefore, you must be careful in using sealing the vein artery techniques. If you are not sure how to revive the person, do not use these techniques.

5. Dim Mak or Tien Hsueh (meridian press or cavity press): 點脈 點穴

As mentioned, the other type of Tien Mie strikes or presses cavities on Chi meridians or channels, and is also called Tien Hsueh (cavity press). Tien means to press with a finger and Hsueh refers to the acupuncture cavities. The human body has more than 800 Chi cavities, mostly on the paths of the eight vessels and 12 channels. Two of the eight vessels are called the Governing and Conception Vessels (Du Mie and Ren Mie). The Chi in these two vessels circulates in a 24 hour cycle. The other 12 Chi channels are related to the 12 internal organs. The flow of Chi in these 12 channels is also related to the time of the day, with the emphasis switching from one channel to the next gradually every 2 hours. Furthermore, these eight vessels and 12 channels also have seasonal and annual cycles. When the Chi circulation in these vessels and channels is stagnant or stopped, the person will sicken or die. Acupuncture is a way to readjust the Chi circulation and cure illnesses.

Cavity press is a method to disturb or affect the opponent's Chi circulation. There are about 108 cavities which can be struck or pressed to affect the Chi flow. Among these 108 cavities, 36 can cause death and the other 72 can cause numbness or unconsciousness. In order to make a strike effective, you must know the time of the major Chi flow (Tzu Wuu Lieu Ju) in that channel, the appropriate striking technique, and the depth of the cavity. We will not go into greater detail in this book, both because it is a very complicated subject, and because it can be very dangerous for a person to learn without supervision. In traditional Chinese martial society, a master will usually not pass these secrets on until he feels he can really trust a student. However, some techniques can be taught without too much danger. These cavities will not cause death, and most are attacked through the method called Jua Hsueh (grabbing the cavity). If you are interested in gaining more knowledge about this, you can read acupuncture books or the author's book: *Chi Kung— Health and Martial Arts*.

Before we finish this section, you should understand that in Chinese martial arts you must have Jing to make your techniques effective. Jing is a way of expressing power which can make the power stronger and more penetrating. When Jing is expressed, the muscles and tendons are supported by the Chi in the body so that the muscles and tendons reach their highest efficiency. Jing can be categorized as hard, soft-hard, or soft. When you apply a Chin Na, regardless of which category it falls into, if you do not know how to use your Jing in the technique your Chin Na will be ineffective. For example, if you do not use Jing in Fen Gin Chin Na, your opponent will have an opportunity to use his muscles to resist your muscles. If you do not use a jerking Jing in Tsuoh Guu Chin Na, you will not be able to break or misplace the opponent's joint. In the same way, in a sealing the breath or cavity press technique, if no Jing is used, the power will not penetrate to the right depth and the technique will be ineffective. For a greater understanding of Jing, refer to the author's book: *Advanced Yang Style Tai Chi Chuan, Vol. 1; Tai Chi Theory and Tai Chi Jing.*

1-3. Learning Chin Na by Yourself

Though it is very hard to catch the Chin Na techniques with 100% accuracy from a book, many techniques can still be learned as long as you ponder, practice, and humbly ask. It cannot be denied that a qualified instructor will help you to shorten the learning time and to catch the keys to each technique. However, if there is no qualified instructor around, then you must rely on yourself.

The first thing to remember when you are teaching yourself is that you should first learn the principle of the technique. This will not only help you to learn that technique, but also to learn other techniques which are based on the same principle. If you thoroughly understand the theory and principles, you will even be able to develop techniques by yourself. Second, after you learn a technique from a book, you should find a partner who is also interested in researching. Discuss the technique and principle with each other. Experiment with it, experience it, become familiar with it, and finally master it. There is no better way than practice, practice, practice. Constant practice makes a technique effective, alive, and natural. You should understand that for a technique to be effective, it must be applied in a natural way as a natural reaction. Only when your reaction is natural and alive can you say that you have grasped the technique.

As you practice Chin Na, learn how much strength you need to do the technique on different people. This can be learned only through practicing with many different types of people. Furthermore, remember when you train your Chin Na that you must train your Yi first. Yi in Chinese means mind. You must put your mind where your technique is, then you can feel if the technique is right, and you will be able to direct your Chi to support the technique. Remember **WHEN YOU USE A CHIN NA, FEELING IS 80% OF THE TECHNIQUE.** You must train your sense of touch so that you know without looking whether your control is effective.

Next, when you practice with a partner be careful to avoid injury. Some injuries can take months to heal completely, and if you are not careful you may even damage your body permanently and give yourself a lifetime of trouble. Therefore, when you practice you must control the power you use on each other. If either of you is in pain, let the other know so he can stop the technique. Unless the other person is your enemy, you do not have to injure him to prove the technique is effective. **PLAY SAFE AND SMART, NOT BRAVE AND STUPID.** You should also learn the basic techniques for dealing with and healing injuries. For example, when a joint is dislocated, what should you do? Chapter 11 will explain basic Chin Na first aid. Please read it carefully.

Keep in mind also that this book shows people standing in particular stances, and doing particular attacks or movements, but when you actually must use the techniques you will probably find that things are quite different. Once you have learned a technique according to the book and can do it easily and effectively, you must experiment with it to find its limits, and how it can be modified. Each technique is designed for particular circumstances, and while it can be modified, there are also circumstances where the technique would be ineffective or even dangerous to you. Also, many times you will start a technique but the opponent will move or counter you, and you will have to modify your technique, or try another one, or even back away. You have not mastered the art until you have learned these things.

One of the common rules of practice is when you apply a technique to your partner, if he is still able to strike back in any way, your technique is wrong. Also, if you cannot use the technique skillfully enough in a practical situation, your technique is useless.

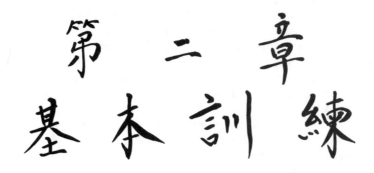

CHAPTER 2
FUNDAMENTAL TRAINING

2-1. Introduction

As in other things, the fundamental training in Chin Na is the root of all the techniques. Without these roots your techniques will be neither powerful, skillful, nor effective. Although the fundamental training in Chin Na may vary from one style to another, the theory and principles remain the same. This means that once you have mastered all the techniques and understand the principles, you might find some fundamental training techniques which are better and more efficient than those in this chapter. Also, you may be able to create another new technique and want to develop some sort of fundamental training to make the techniques more effective.

Chin Na techniques can generally be classified as Small Circle (Shao Jiuan), Medium Circle (Jong Jiuan), or Large Circle (Da Jiuan) Chin Na. Techniques applied to the fingers or wrists are called Small Circle Chin Na, while techniques for controlling the elbow are considered Medium Circle Chin Na. When a technique is used on the elbow and shoulder along with stepping, it is called Large Circle Chin Na.

In this chapter we will introduce training exercises which are used for all three circles. These exercises are commonly used in White Crane, Tiger, and Eagle styles. As mentioned, once you understand the principles, you should be able to devise other training methods which are more appropriate to your own style.

After you have gone through the exercises in this chapter, go on to learn the Chin Na techniques. Once you have learned the techniques, come back to this chapter to train again, and place emphasis on the sense of having an opponent in front of you when you are doing the fundamental training. This will help you to understand the purpose of each exercise.

All the basic training has both offensive and defensive purposes. In offense you want to control your opponent, while in defense you want to escape from your opponent's attack, and hopefully to counterattack him. In order to either use your Chin Na effectively or to escape and counterattack easily, you must train five things. The first is Li (muscular power). Some muscular strength is needed both to do the techniques and to maintain control. Second is Chi. Chi is an internal energy which comes from the concentration of your Yi (mind). When you concentrate, your Chi will reach the muscles being used and increase their efficiency. Third is Jing. Slow Jing is a mixture of Li and Chi, in which Li plays the major role, but with fast Jing, muscle become less important than Chi. A jerking motion is necessary to generate a sharp, penetrating power which can be used for cavity strike, misplacing the joints, or breaking bones. Fourth is speed. Without speed, you will not be able to use your techniques because your opponent will be able to sense you easily and escape from your attempt. The last important requirement is skill. Even if you have the above four elements, if you do not have a high degree of skill, you will still not be able to control your opponent.

From the above discussion it is clear that the training consists of two major elements: physical and mental. Physical training includes the strength and speed of the muscles, tendons, and ligaments. Mental training is concerned with the training of Chi (internal energy), Yi (mind concentration), Shen (spirit), feeling, and reactions. Since many of the exercises discussed below train several of these at the same time, we will not discuss the training of each element individually. For example, when you train your physical strength, you must also train your concentration and reactions.

Furthermore, it is very difficult to discuss this training by dividing it into different exercises for the fingers, wrist, arms, and so on. When you train, you are not working on the power and speed of only one specific area, but rather you are training the whole of your body to act in a coordinated and effective manner. That means that when you train your fingers, you are also training at least your wrist and arm. Nonetheless, in this chapter we will discuss the parts of the body individually to focus your attention more carefully on their functions, and we will present exercises to help you train and understand each part. Please keep in mind, however, that **FOR MAXIMUM EFFECTIVENESS EACH TECHNIQUE MUST UTILIZE THE WHOLE BODY.**

2-2. Speed and Power Training

Speed is the most important factor in an effective Chin Na technique. With many Chin Na you need to use only one-half or even one-third of the power of your opponent. However, without speed you will not be able to control your opponent before he escapes or reacts against you. There are many other Chin Na which do require considerable power to execute the technique and to maintain control. If you do not have the necessary speed and power your Chin Na will remain second rate, and you will often find that you have exposed yourself to counterattack or otherwise put yourself in a disadvantageous position. Therefore, speed and power are a major part of the training in a Chin Na course.

In order to make the grabbing Chin Na effective you must first train your grabbing speed and power. This training will include: finger and palm speed and power, arm extension and twisting speed and power, using the waist to direct the Jing to your arms and fingers, and stepping to set up the advantageous position for your technique. In all, an effective Chin Na requires speed, power, and the coordination of arms, waist, and stepping.

A. Finger Grabbing Speed:
1. Finger Closing:

Finger closing training is easy to practice, and can be done almost

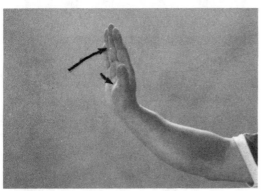

Figure 2-1.

Figure 2-2.

Figure 2-3.

Figure 2-4.

anytime and anywhere. To practice, hold your hand out with the fingers pointing up (Figure 2-1) and simply close your fingers as if you were grabbing something, until your fingers touch the center of your palm (Figure 2-2), and then open immediately. In the beginning, close your fingers 180 times in 30 seconds, and gradually increase the count. The record is 300 times in 30 seconds.

In Finger Chin Na techniques the thumb and first two fingers play the major role. White Crane uses a training exercise called Crane Claw Grabbing (Huo Jao Jua) which specializes in training the thumb in coordination with the first two fingers. It is similar to the Finger Closing training discussed above, except that you use only the thumb and first two fingers (Figures 2-3 and 2-4).

2. Finger Waving:

Finger waving trains the base of the fingers, i.e., the palm. There are two such exercises used in White Crane. One is palm bending training, called Flying Wing (Fei Chyh) training, and the other uses a waving motion and is called Finger Wave (Jyy Bo) training.

In Flying Wing training, hold your hand out with the fingers up (Figure 2-5), then bend all your fingers forward except your thumb (Figure 2-6) and straighten them up again. It will look like a bird waving its wing. Also try 180 times in 30 seconds in the beginning, and gradually increase the repetitions.

In Finger Wave training you bend your fingers forward one after the other except your thumb (Figure 2-7), and then straighten them immediately, one after the other (Figure 2-8). Practice starting both with

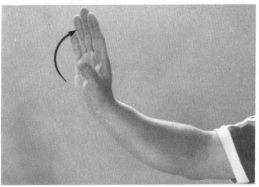

Figure 2-5.

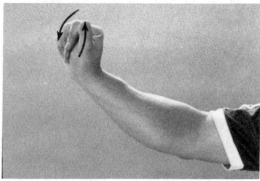

Figure 2-6.

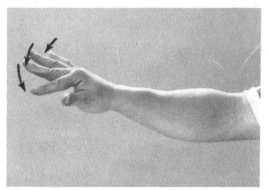

Figure 2-7.

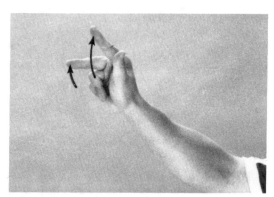

Figure 2-8.

the index finger and with the little finger, so that you can do it in either direction. Your fingers motion will look like an ocean wave. Try 100 times in 30 seconds at first, and gradually increase the repetitions.

3. Picking up Coins:

Finger speed alone is not enough to make your grabbing Chin Na effective—you also need to be able to coordinate the movement of your arm with the action of your fingers. A good exercise for developing this is picking up coins. To do this, first lay out about fifty coins at random on a table, and stand so that your arm must be fully extended to reach the furthest coin. Reach out and pick up a coin and put it in your other hand (Figure 2-9). Repeat the process with all the coins, picking them up one at a time and putting them individually into your other hand. The object is to pick them all up as fast as possible. This exercise trains not only the speed and coordination of your fingers and arms, but also develops your concentration and accuracy.

A common way for people to compare speed and reaction time is for one person to hold a coin in his open hand, palm up, and another person to try to grab the coin out of his hand before he closes it.

4. Picking Leaves:

This practice is similar to picking coins. Grab individual leaves by their base, break them off and place them in your other hand. You must be quick and accurate, and you must not crush or damage the leaves. Do this for thirty seconds and then count the leaves you have picked. Gradually work at increasing the number of leaves. This exercise is much harder than picking up coins because leaves grow at all different angles.

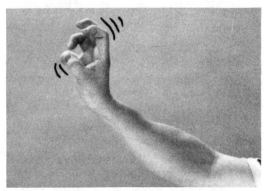

Figure 2-10.

Figure 2-9.

B. Finger Grabbing Power:

Although finger strength is not so important in Finger Chin Na, it will be very important in other Chin Na in which you must grab the wrist, arm, or muscle. As with speed training, we will present exercises emphasizing individual parts of the body, although in these exercises you will in fact be training more than just that part.

1. Grabbing Air:

Many styles of Chinese martial arts have their own air grabbing training. The main purpose of this exercise is to train the practitioner's Yi (mind), for it is the concentrated mind which generates Chi to support the muscles so they can function at their highest efficiency. This training is similar to Da Mo's Yi Gin Ching (Muscle Change Classic) in Wai Dan Chi Kung training (see the author's book: *Chi Kung—Health and Martial Arts*). Repeated training will increase your concentration and strengthen your Chi and Jing.

In this section we will discuss exercises which are used by the Tiger, Eagle, and White Crane styles. The practitioners of these styles are famous for having very strong hands. This is due in part to the hand forms they use, because certain hand forms are particularly good for developing the Chi in the hands and strengthening them. (See the discussion of Chi and hand forms in the author's book: *Advanced Yang Style Tai Chi Chuan, Vol. 1, Tai Chi theory and Tai Chi Jing*).

Tiger style: When this style grabs, the hand imitates the tiger's paw (Figure 2-10) to generate Chi in the hands. With your hand open, concentrate on your fingers and gradually close them from knuckle to knuckle until your hand forms a tight fist (Figure 2-11). Open your hand and repeat the same process (Figure 2-12). When practicing, stand in Ma Bu (horse stance), keep your mind calm, your root firm, and your breathing uniform. Cross your hands in front of your chest (Figure 2-13), turn your palms forward and at the same time make a grabbing motion (Figures 2-14 and 2-15). Tiger style practitioners start with 50 repetitions every morning, facing the rising sun. Exhale every time you grab, and inhale when you open your hands and withdraw them to your chest to repeat the process. Practice until you can do 100 repetitions every morning.

Figure 2-11.

Figure 2-12.

Figure 2-13.

Figure 2-14.

Figure 2-15.

Eagle style: This style imitates the eagle's strong claw (Figure 2-16) to generate a clawing type of strength. Typical Eagle claw grabbing training consists of standing in Ma Bu and extending your right arm in a screwing motion and grabbing with a claw hand, palm facing left (Figures 2-17 and 2-18). Pull your arm back to your waist and extend your other arm, repeating the same process.

Crane style: This is similar to Eagle claw training except that the grabbing is done with a Crane claw (Figure 2-19), and when you grab your palm faces forward (Figures 2-20 and 2-21).

2. Branch or Spring Grabbing:

Many styles use equipment for developing power in grabbing training. The most common way in China is to practice grabbing the upper part of a Y shaped branch. These days it is possible to buy a spring in sports stores which will serve the purpose perfectly (Figure 2-22). Remember **WHEN YOU TRAIN THAT YOU MUST CONCENTRATE INTENSELY IN ORDER TO GENERATE THE CHI TO SUPPORT THE MUSCLES.**

3. Finger Pushups:

There are two types of finger pushups, one develops strength and the other endurance. To develop strength, start with 20 repetitions and

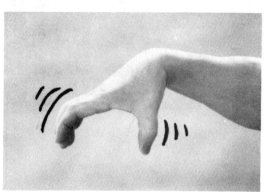

Figure 2-16.

Figure 2-17.

Figure 2-18.

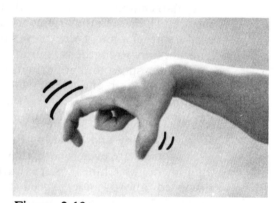

Figure 2-19.

Figure 2-20.

Figure 2-21.

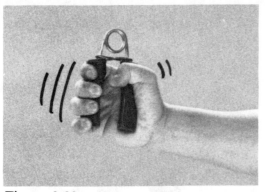

Figure 2-22.

Figure 2-23.

gradually increase the number. Once you can do 50 easily, start keeping your little fingers up so that you are doing the pushups on four fingers of each hand. As your finger strength increases, stop using your ring fingers, and then your middle fingers, and finally your index fingers, so that you are doing the pushups on your thumbs.

Once you are able to do twenty pushups on all your fingers, you should also train clapping. To do this, when you lift yourself clap your hands and then return them to the original positions. Once you can do this ten times easily, start clapping twice or even three times each time your lift yourself. This not only strengthens your muscles, tendons, and ligaments, but also trains your speed and coordination.

To train your endurance with finger pushups, remain in the low position (Figure 2-23) for 2 minutes. Gradually increase the time to develop the endurance of your muscles, ligament, and tendons.

4. Air Twisting and Breaking Branches:

Since trees are everywhere, they used to be the most common training equipment for Chinese martial artists. In addition to the leaf picking discussed above under speed training, martial artists also twisted branches to strengthen their fingers, wrists, and arms. When you train, start with smaller branches and gradually increase the size as your strength increases. As you train you will notice that equal sized branches from different kinds of trees will vary greatly in their resistance to breaking. Remember **WHEN YOU BEGIN TRAINING TO PROCEED SLOWLY AND CAREFULLY, GRADUALLY BUILDING UP YOUR STRENGTH AND TOUGHENING YOUR SKIN.** Increase speed slowly and be careful to avoid injury. It is best if you only start this training after you have practiced air twisting and coordinating your Yi with your finger muscles. Only when you feel comfortable with all the hand forms should you start practicing on branches. The training here is from the Crane style, and the hand forms will imitate the crane's wing.

    a. Left Twisting: When you do the air twisting exercises stand with both feet parallel. This stance is usually used in Kung Fu training for several reasons. First, when your feet are parallel you are more stable than when you are standing in a casual, everyday position. Second, when your feet are parallel the outsides of your ankles are slightly stretched. This generates Chi there, and this Chi helps you to build your root. Third, when your feet are parallel the cavities or striking points located on the inside of your legs are better protected. This is especially desirable because the cavities on the inside of your legs are generally more vulnerable than the cavities on the outside.

Figure 2-24.

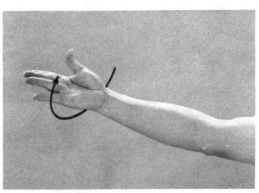

Figure 2-25.

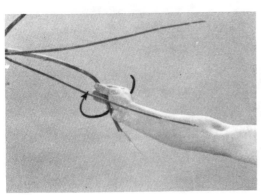

Figure 2-26.

Figure 2-27.

When you train air twisting, stare at a point far in front of you. This will help you to concentrate and to extend your Yi further. Next, concentrate on your fingers, wrists, and then on your arms, which do most of the twisting. Ultimately, your whole body will be involved in the technique (Figures 2-24 and 2-25). After you practice a while, you will find that the areas you are training become warm, which means that Chi is flowing, and eventually you will find your twisting strength increasing significantly.

After you have practiced air twisting for several months, start twisting branches (Figure 2-26). Start with thin ones and gradually increase the thickness. Practice slowly at first and later gradually increase your speed. Remember: **PRACTICE WITH INTELLIGENCE, NOT YOUR EGO.**

b. Right Twisting: This training is similar to the previous one. The air twisting form is shown in Figure 2-27, with the hand action detailed in Figure 2-28. The branch twisting training is shown in Figure 2-29.

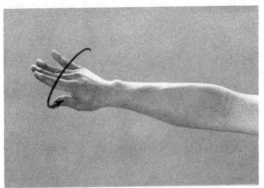

Figure 2-28.

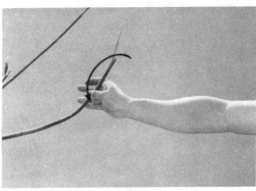

Figure 2-29.

Figure 2-30.

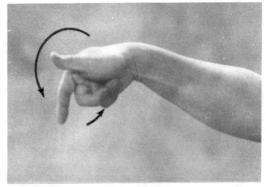

Figure 2-31.

c. Pressing Twisting: The pressing twisting form is shown in Figure 2-30, with the hand form detailed in Figure 2-31. It is hard to figure out the technique just from looking at the hand form, but when you see what it does to the branch you will easily understand its purpose (Figure 2-32).

d. Hooking Twisting: This exercise specializes in training the little finger and the fourth finger in hooking. The air twisting hand form is shown in Figures 2-33 and 2-34. The branch training is shown in Figures 2-35 and 2-36.

You should understand that all of the above twisting exercises are the foundation of finger Chin Na. When you can perform them skillfully and smoothly you will have grasped the key to success. Naturally, you do not need to have real branches to do this training. Once you understand the idea of the training, you can easily design training aids for yourself which will help you to achieve the same purpose.

5. Stone Lock or Brick Grabbing:

The stone lock is a very common training aid in the Chinese martial arts, especially in the Southern styles which emphasize hand techniques. A stone lock (Shyr Suoo) is a stone shaped like a Chinese lock (Figure 2-37), usually weighing from 30 to 60 pounds. The stone lock is generally

Figure 2-32.

Figure 2-33.

Figure 2-34.

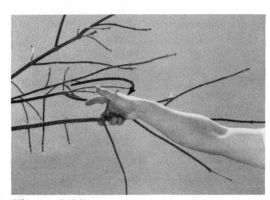

Figure 2-35.

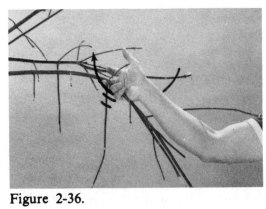

Figure 2-36.

Figure 2-37.

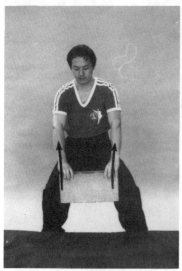

Figure 2-38.   Figure 2-39.   Figure 2-40.

used to train catching speed, strength, and the coordination of fingers, wrist, and arm. The practitioner swings the lock, throws it up in the air so that it spins, and then catches it by the handle. There are many training techniques, but since stone locks are not readily available in the Western world, we will not go into the training here.

However, even without a stone lock, you can still use the same principles with a brick to train your grabbing and catching speed and power.

In brick grabbing training, use a brick which weighs about 20 pounds, and whose width is appropriate to your grip. There are several methods of training:

a. Drop Grabbing: Drop grabbing is the easiest way to train with a brick. Stand in a Horse Stance and hold the brick in front of you (Figure 2-38). Lift the brick and then drop it, catching the brick with both hands before it hits the ground (Figure 2-39). When you are used to the weight, use a heavier brick, up to 50 pounds or more.

b. Drop and Clap Grabbing: To develop speed and coordination in extending your arms, add another exercise as you increase the weight. This exercise is similar to drop grabbing except that after you drop the brick, clap your hands before you catch the brick. Once you can do this easily, either increase the number of claps or increase the weight.

c. Up-Down and Side Rotation Grabbing: This training is even harder than the drop and clap training. In this exercise, rotate the brick forward or backward (Figure 2-40), or sidewards either clockwise or counterclockwise (Figures 2-41 and 2-42) right before you drop it. It is harder to catch the brick when it is falling at these different angles. Start this exercise only when you have developed the strength of your fingers, wrists, and arms, then you can practice turning the brick to every possible angle.

In brick dropping training, once you have mastered catching the brick with both hands, you should then repeat the same training using only one hand. After you have mastered both two hand and single hand training, you should then grease or polish the brick so that it is slippery. This will increase your grabbing capability significantly.

Figure 2-41.   Figure 2-42.   Figure 2-43.

C. Wrist Twisting Training:

If you have strong fingers but weak wrists and arms, even when you grab your opponent, he can still easily reverse the situation. Therefore, the second part of your training should emphasize wrist strength, especially twisting power.

1. Staff and Swinging Weight Training:

Using a staff is probably the easiest and most effective way to train the endurance and twisting power of your wrists. In staff training, you simply grasp the staff by its end and hold it extended. If you find this too difficult, hold it closer to the center. Let the other end of the staff fall and use the power of your wrist to stop it (Figure 2-43), then use the strength of your wrist to raise and lower the other end of the staff. Start with 30 repetitions, and gradually increase the length of time you hold the staff extended, and the number of repetitions. When you can do 50 repetitions in a short period of time, start swinging the far end of the staff sidewards (Figure 2-44) or in a circle (Figure 2-45). You should also work at moving your arm in a half circle (Figure 2-46) or whole circle (Figure 2-47) clockwise and counterclockwise while keeping the far end of the staff still.

When you find that all the available staffs are too light for you, then you can start swinging weight training. This is usually done with a three foot long stick which has a five to ten pound weight attached to the end with a rope. The weight can be increased to suit you, though the inertia that the weight develops as it swings adds a lot to its effective weight. To do this exercise, stand with the feet well apart and hold the stick at one end. In the first exercise, lift the weight up without raising your wrist and then let the stick drop, stopping it at the horizontal with a sudden tensing of your wrist (Figure 2-48). This exercise is similar to when your opponent pulls you, and you stop him with a sudden tensing of your wrist. The second exercise consists of moving the tip of the stick from side to side without letting either the weight or your hand change position (Figure 2-49). Next move the end you are holding from side to side while keeping the weight and the tip of the stick stationary (Figure 2-50). Finally, keep the tip of the stick and the weight stationary and move the hand in a three foot circle both clockwise and counterclockwise (Figure 2-51). This develops strength and suppleness in the arm.

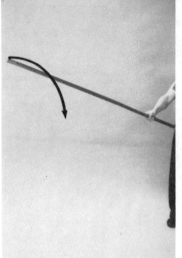

Figure 2-44.

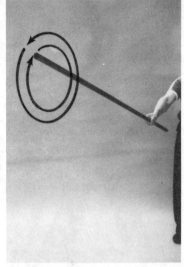

Figure 2-45.

Figure 2-46.

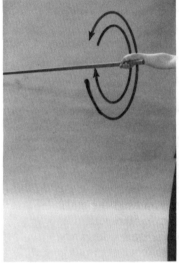

Figure 2-47.

Figure 2-48.

Figure 2-49.

Figure 2-50.

Figure 2-51.

Figure 2-52.

Figure 2-53.

Figure 2-54.

2. Windlass:

This exercise is done using a five to ten pound weight suspended with a cord from the center of a short wooden bar. Stand with the feet well apart and hold the bar straight out at shoulder level. Wind the cord onto the bar, thereby lifting the weight as far as it will go. Lower the weight by unwinding the cord; continue winding the cord to lift the weight again, then lower it to the floor. Increase the number of windings within a limited time period. This set should be performed both with the hands held palm down as in Figure 2-52, and with the hands held palm up as in Figure 2-53.

D. Arm Twisting and Extending Training:

In addition to the strength of your fingers and wrists, you must also have strong arms. The success of your control in grabbing Chin Na depends upon the speed with which you can extend your arm, and your twisting power. Many techniques require that you use your arm to twist some part of the opponent, and so your speed and power in this will determine your success in seizing and holding the opponent in position. Your speed in extending your arm is also extremely important for both grabbing and striking Chin Na.

1. Weight Drop:

Weight drop is an exercise which trains the arm's extending speed and strength. You should understand that there are two kinds of muscles in your body, one deals with strength and the other with speed. Very often when you over-emphasize one you will hinder the other. The best exercise will let you train both power and speed at the same time.

In weight drop training, you simply use a rope to hang a weight from your elbow (Figure 2-54). Then extend your arm completely (Figure 2-55) and withdraw it back to its original bent position. Try 50 times first and if you find that it is too easy, increase the weight and/or shorten the time. Remember, in all your training use common sense and be careful. Increase weights and speed gradually so that you develop your body rather than strain it. Fast and careless training only causes injury.

2. Panther Walk:

Panther walk training develops the arms and shoulders so that they will

Figure 2-55.

Figure 2-56.

Figure 2-57.

Figure 2-58.

be strong and fast like a panther's. This exercise is very simple. Get into the pushup position with your elbows bent and your legs straight. Push up and backward with both arms so that your body hops forward (Figure 2-56). You can also hop backward the same way (Figure 2-57), or sideways (Figure 2-58). Keep your arms close to your body rather than extended outward. Practice hopping 25 feet forward, backward, to the right, and to the left. Once your arms and shoulders become stronger, increase speed and distance. This exercise develops the speed and strength of your arm's extending and resisting, which is important for holding the opponent in a steady position in a Chin Na control. Someday if you find your fingers are strong enough, you can then train the same way on your fingers instead of on your hands, which will then also develop your fingers (Figure 2-59).

Once you can do the above exercises easily, you can then imitate the panther's walk. Keep your arms bent and close to your body (Figure 2-60). This training is harder than the above one. The disadvantage of this training is that it will build the power muscles and slow you down.

3. Arm Twisting Training:

There are several ways to train arm twisting. One common way is called Bamboo Bundle (Jwu Ba) training, although sometimes rattan is used instead of bamboo. Tie together a bundle of bamboo or rattan rods about four feet long. You and your partner hold the ends and swing in opposite

Figure 2-59.

Figure 2-60.

Figure 2-61.

Figure 2-62.

directions (Figures 2-61 and 2-62). At first, one person holds tight when swinging to one side and slightly loose when swinging to the other side. The other person does the same but in the opposite directions. When you swing, the end of the bundle will spread out and you must hold it together. This training toughens the skin of your palms, develops the strength of your grip, and practices the twisting motion of your arms. Once you and your partner have toughened your hands, hold the bundle tightly throughout the exercise.

One way to compete with the bamboo bundles is to have one person tightly hold one end stationary while the other one swings his end and spins his body in one or more circles (Figure 2-63). Whoever loosens his grip loses.

4. Breaking Training

Sometimes grabbing Chin Na will break or dislocate one of the opponent's bones or joints. This is hard to do if you just use your muscles. There are two reasons for this. First, because muscular power is dull and slow, your opponent can easily sense your intention, and then tighten his muscles to resist you. Second, muscular power is shallow, so unless you are very strong your power will have difficulty penetrating to your opponent's bones. For these reasons an advanced Chin Na practitioner will always use jerking Jing to do the job. Jerking Jing is normally generated by the legs and directed by the waist to express the power through the arms and hands. Jerking Jing is deep, penetrating, and powerful. Once you have set up the right angle for a Chin Na, if you know how to generate Jing and apply it in the technique, you can usually

Figure 2-63.

Figure 2-64.

control your opponent easily with little power. If you desire, you can also use the Jing to break the joint or tear the muscles instantly and cause your opponent permanent damage. Jing training is extremely important in Chinese martial arts. It is almost impossible to discuss the principle and the idea of Jing in a few paragraphs or even several chapters. If you are interested in Jing, please refer to the author's book: *Advanced Yang Style Tai Chi Chuan, Vol. 1, Tai Chi Theory and Tai Chi Jing*.

For Jing breaking training you simply hold a thin tree branch, generate power from your root, and direct it to your arms to break the branch in a quick, sharp movement (Figure 2-64). Use the same movements as in the Air Twisting and Branch Breaking exercises of the finger power training section above. Once you can do this, increase the thickness of the branch. When you train to use your Jing in breaking, your Yi (mind) must concentrate on the arm and hand. When one flow of Chi reaches the Dan Tien, the other balanced flow of Chi reaches the hands to do the job.

E. Coiling Training:

Coiling training is also very important for training grabbing Chin Na, for if you know how to coil you can reach the right joint and set up the correct angle for the technique. It is important to use the correct angle because then you will need significantly less power. Furthermore, good coiling will help you to adhere to the opponent with your hands so that he cannot escape. For these reasons, coiling training has become a major emphasis in the training of Southern and internal styles.

There are two coiling exercises, which you can train with a staff or even your own arm. The first one is downward coiling. Place your wrist on the staff, and coil the side of your hand downward around the staff (Figures 2-65 and 2-66). If you don't have a staff, you can hold one arm out and coil the other around it in the same way (Figure 2-67). The second coiling training is sideward. Use the side of your hand and your wrist to coil around a staff either clockwise or counterclockwise (Figures 2-68 and 2-69).

F. Stepping Training:

Stepping plays an important role, especially in medium and large circle Chin Na. Stepping can help you to set up the most advantageous position to use your technique, and can also help you to pull the opponent's root

Figure 2-65.

Figure 2-66.

Figure 2-67.

Figure 2-68.

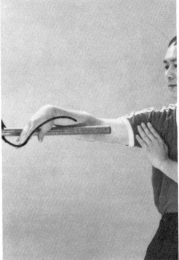

Figure 2-69.

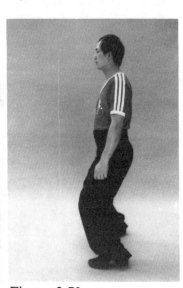

Figure 2-70.

and put him into a defenseless situation.

We will only introduce a few examples of stepping training. In the following chapters, whenever you find it is necessary to train your stepping for a specific technique, you should do so.

1. Forward and Up:

Forward and up is a stepping for setting up a forward Chin Na control. Usually you use this stepping to uproot or lift the opponent so his heels are off the ground. To train this stepping, start in a low stance such as the horse stance, and step forward with the right leg as you raise your body (Figures 2-70 and 2-71). As you train, imagine that you are lifting a heavy object, and remember that you must push downward first in order to generate an upward force.

2. Backward and Down:

Backward and down is the exact opposite of the last stepping exercise. In this stepping, you want to pull your opponent to your rear and side and

Figure 2-71.

Figure 2-72.

Figure 2-73.

Figure 2-74.

Figure 2-75.

Figure 2-76

bring him to the ground. In this application you usually want at least your opponent's elbow to touch the ground. Start this exercise in a horse stance, and step the right leg backward into a four-six stance as you also bend your body slightly forward (Figures 2-72 and 2-73).

3. Sideways and Slide:

Sideways and slide is used to set up and control the opponent from the side. While you are stepping sideways you usually also want to either lift your opponent up or force him down. In this exercise, you usually step one of your feet to the opponent's side and drag your other foot with it to the side (Figures 2-74 and 2-75).

4. Sideways and Circle:

Sideways and circle is used whenever you want your opponent to lose his balance and root. This is common in large circle Chin Na. In this stepping exercise, step one of your feet to the side of your opponent and immediately follow with the other foot, and finally twist your body to pull the opponent around and off balance. Figures 2-76, 2-77, and 2-78 show

Figure 2-77.

Figure 2-78.

Figure 2-79.

Figure 2-80.

the circle to the right while Figures 2-79 and 2-80 show the circle to the left.

2-3. General Rules for Grabbing Chin Na Control

Remember one thing. When you use a grabbing Chin Na on an opponent, you are showing him mercy. If you can control him with a grabbing Chin Na, you can strike or kick him more easily and more safely. There are two circumstances under which you would use a grabbing Chin Na in a fight. The first is when you are using sticking and adhering techniques, and grabbing Chin Na can be used easily and effectively. The second is when your fighting ability is much higher than your opponent's, and you do not want to injure him. You demonstrate your Chin Na on him to show mercy and to prove to him that you have the ability to control him.

Once you have decided to use your grabbing Chin Na, you must control him completely. Half-way control will only bring you trouble and danger. There are a few general rules which you should remember:

1. When you apply a lifting Chin Na, you must lift your opponent's heels off the floor. Otherwise, he will still have his root and he will be able to punch or kick you.
2. When you use a downward Chin Na, you must bring him down so his face or elbow touches the ground, and he is completely defenseless. Remember: **TO SHOW MERCY TO YOUR ENEMY IS TO BE CRUEL TO YOURSELF.**
3. When you use a circular Chin Na, you must destroy your opponent's balance and pull his root. His root and balance give him the ability to resist and counterattack. Once he has lost his root, you can then control him either downward or upward.
4. When you apply a Chin Na control to an opponent, you should always have a backup technique such as a punch or kick so that you can destroy his capacity to fight if your Chin Na control fails. If you see that you need to hit him, do not hesitate.
5. Whatever Chin Na you do, do not turn your body in front of your opponent. Set him up in an awkward position first, then you can turn either on his side or behind him. Turning in front of your opponent without first putting him in a disadvantageous position is extremely dangerous and unwise.
6. The key words of grabbing Chin Na are **TWIST, BEND, and PRESS.**

2-4. Chin Na Escape Training

A Chin Na expert must also know how to escape from an opponent's Chin Na control, and be able to counterattack and reverse the situation. To escape from an opponent's control you must master several techniques in addition to those explained in the previous section. One of the major techniques is knowing how to sense the angle at which your opponent is grabbing, and being able to change the angle so that his control of your muscles and joint is ineffective. This will give you time to escape. Of course, often you will be able to escape if you struggle and sweat a bit. However, for a skillful escape the most important factor is speed, and the second is skill. Power is not so important in an escape as it is in offensive Chin Na. In this section, we will first introduce general ideas on how to escape, and follow this with some exercises.

1. Rotation Escape:

The main reason for rotation when you are grabbed is to change the angle of the grab. When your opponent grabs you, he will try to do it at the most effective angle and location. In order to escape you must act immediately. If you cannot rotate and change the situation before he has completed his control, you have lost. It is therefore extremely important to thoroughly practice escapes both by yourself and with a partner.

When you neutralize an opponent's grabbing attack, it is important to remember to neutralize it in such a way that he cannot immediately continue his attack with another technique. Usually, when you rotate out of a grab you will pull your hand back as soon as possible, but while you do so you must be prepared to deal with a possible punch if your opponent tries to continue his attack.

Solo escape practice is very simple, and you may use almost all of the escape techniques. You simply use one hand to apply the technique to the other hand, and practice the escape with the grabbed hand. Solo practice has the limitation that, since you know and expect the technique, you cannot build up much sensitivity. It is therefore necessary to also practice with a partner.

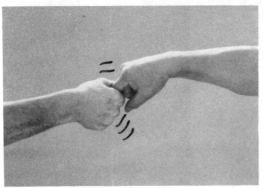
Figure 2-81.

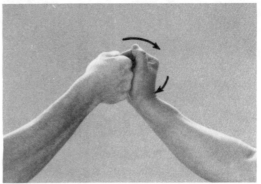
Figure 2-82.

2. Pressure Release Escape:

Pressure release escape is the natural reaction of your body to pain. The principle is very simple. When your opponent tries to control you with Chin Na, before he completes his control you simply use your other hand to grab the opponent's fingers or hand which is causing you the pain. This pressure release technique is commonly used in Chin Na counterattack. In this case, right after you have released the pressure, immediately change your grab into a Chin Na technique. Therefore, pressure release escape can be practiced only with a partner.

3. Distraction Escape:

Distraction escape is probably the easiest and most effective technique among the three. Before your opponent has completed his control, you simply distract his concentration, for example by kicking his shin or groin. Alternatively, you can use the other hand to punch his nose or poke his eyes. When his attention is unfocused, you immediately escape from his grab and, if possible, counterattack with a Chin Na of your own.

Distraction is very effective in Chin Na, and it is commonly used both in offense and defense. In offense, you will often find that your opponent tenses his muscles right after you grab him. This makes it very hard for you to continue your technique. When this happens, simply punch or kick him to distract him, and immediately apply a Chin Na. Remember that **CHIN NA IS EFFECTIVE ONLY WHEN IT IS A SURPRISE.**

It would be very hard to say which technique is the most effective escape. As a matter of fact, it depends on the situation and the technique being used. It is impossible to discuss escapes for every technique here. However, once you understand the principles and have practiced a lot with your partners, you will soon find that escaping is much easier than controlling. Once you thoroughly understand a technique, you should already understand the escape.

Example 1. Finger Escape:

Finger escape is used to escape from a finger Chin Na. To use a finger Chin Na you must keep the opponent's finger straight so that you can lock it in position and bend it. Once you realize this, you can see that when someone tries to apply a finger Chin Na on you, you must react quickly and bend your finger and close your fist to protect the rest of the fingers. The trick to bending the trapped finger is not to try to bend that finger itself, or pull it out of his grasp, but rather to move your palm to the trapped finger. Your should also close the other fingers to protect them, and rotate and pull your arm back (Figures 2-81 and 2-82). To practice,

Figure 2-83.

Figure 2-84.

Figure 2-85.

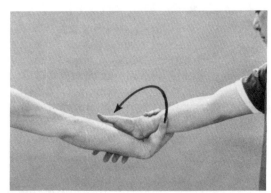

Figure 2-86.

have your partner grab your fingers so you can work out escapes from the various positions. You must build up your reactions so that whenever you feel you are in danger you will react automatically.

Example 2. Wrist Escapes:

Wrist locks play a major role in Chin Na, and it is important to learn how to escape from them and to effectively counterattack. In principle, it is very easy to escape from a wrist grab. In practice, however, it is not always quite so easy, because your opponent usually knows what escapes and counters are possible, and is prepared for them. Therefore, in order to escape successfully you must have fast reactions. **YOU MUST REACT BEFORE THE CONTROL IS COMPLETED**, for once it is completed, it is too late to do anything.

There are a few reactions which you must train until they become natural. The first is to escape through the gap between the thumb and index finger. When your opponent grabs you (Figure 2-83), there is a gap between his thumb and index finger. Therefore, once you sense your wrist is being grabbed, tense your arm and rotate and redirect it to the gap either clockwise (Figure 2-84) or counterclockwise (Figure 2-85). If you are not completely controlled yet, this motion will hinder the opponent. When you have done this, you should immediately rotate your wrist and coil your hand onto his wrist (Figures 2-86 and 2-87). This will set his wrist in an awkward angle for further controlling and also set him up for your counterattack. Alternatively, before you are completely controlled you can immediately tense up your wrist muscles and straighten your arm so that it is in a line with the opponent's arm (Figure 2-88). This puts the opponent at a disadvantageous angle for further control. For wrist escape

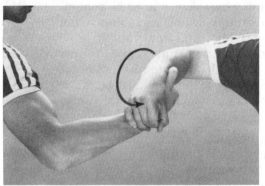

Figure 2-87.

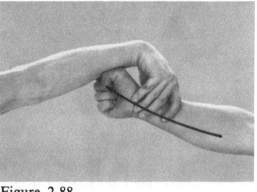

Figure 2-88.

Figure 2-89.

Figure 2-90.

self-practice, you can use one hand to grab the other wrist and escape in different ways (Figures 2-89 and 2-90).

In addition to the above escape principles, there are a few tricks which will help you to escape easily. First, when your wrist is grabbed, use the other hand to punch his face or else kick his shin to distract his attention and disturb his focus on your wrist. Then you can easily escape. Next, when you escape, if you know how to generate Jing from your legs, you can always injure the opponent's wrist unless he lets go before your Jing reaches his wrist.

Example 3. Arm Rotation Escapes:

It is usually easier to escape from an arm Chin Na than from a wrist Chin Na. This is because your arm is stronger and thicker than your wrist, and therefore harder to control. However, many Chin Na do attack the arm, most commonly by grabbing the wrist and the elbow at the same time. When this happens, do not consider that you are grabbed in two places, but rather simply treat it as if only your wrist were being grabbed, and react as appropriate for a wrist control. This will work because your elbow is stronger than your wrist, and once you can free your wrist your opponent will not be able to hold your elbow by itself.

2-5. General Rules for Countering a Grabbing Chin Na

Generally speaking, it is harder to counterattack against a grabbing Chin Na than it is to attack with a grabbing Chin Na. This is because when you attack you make the decision what technique to apply, whereas when you counterattack you are responding to another person's attack, and your actions are determined by, and limited by, the technique he applies. Therefore, in order to be able to counterattack against a grabbing Chin Na you must know what your opponent is doing and what your possible actions are. Not only that, it normally takes less than one second to apply a Chin Na, so you have probably one third of that time to react. In order for you to react naturally and skillfully, your technique must be much higher than the attacker's. There are a few rules which you should always remember:

1. Always consider escape first and counter second. You must save yourself first before you can counterattack. It cannot be denied that sometimes a counterattack is the best way to escape. However, you should train yourself to escape first, and once you have developed your reactions enough you will find yourself counterattacking naturally when it is appropriate.

2. If you are not sure you can use a grabbing Chin Na for your counterattack, do not use it. Punching or kicking counterattacks are much easier, faster, and safer than grabbing Chin Na.

3. When you use a counterattack, you must react before you are completely controlled. You should understand that a perfect grabbing Chin Na control is very fast and effective when done by a Chin Na expert. Once you are controlled completely, you will not have any chance to escape.

Since there are many possible counter techniques to use against each grabbing Chin Na, it is impossible to describe all of them in this book. We will only introduce one of the possible counterattacks for each technique, and this counter might not be the best one. This is because we wish to show you as many counterattacks as possible, and to avoid frequent repetition of certain techniques. This variety should also help to deepen your understanding of counterattacking. It is quite possible that you will find a counter for a particular technique which is much better than the one described in this book.

CHAPTER 3
FINGER CHIN NA

In ancient times, almost every grabbing Chin Na had a name. This was to help the student remember the more than one hundred techniques. We would like to give you the names of all the techniques we present, but there are two problems. First, even though most of the techniques have been preserved, many of the names have been forgotten due to the decline of the martial arts in the last hundred years. Second, many of the techniques have many names because they are used in several different styles. In order to help you remember the techniques, we will give names for all of them. If one has several names, we will pick one, and if the name has been forgotten, we will create one. If you chose, you can even name them for yourself.

3-1. Introduction

Before we discuss finger Chin Na techniques, you should understand that fingers are the most important weapon for both you and your opponent. Without fingers you cannot grasp. If your opponent loses the use of his fingers he will lose the ability to fight. It stands to reason that finger Chin Na has been extensively developed in many styles. As mentioned, when Chin Na is applied to the fingers or wrists, it is usually called Small Circle (Shao Jiuan), while techniques which control the elbow are called Medium Circle (Jong Jiuan). When Chin Na is used on the elbow and shoulder along with stepping, it is called Large Circle (Da Jiuan).

There are some advantages and some disadvantages to finger Chin Na. The advantages are: 1. It is effective. It does not matter how big or strong a person is, once his finger is locked correctly, you only need a slight force to control him easily. Sometimes you will encounter people who are double jointed. Either through natural ability or extensive stretching a person may be able to bend his hand forward and touch his fingers to his forearm. It is very difficult to apply wrist Chin Na to such a person, but if you can lock one of his fingers, you will be able to control him easily. 2. When finger Chin Na is applied, it is fast. You can often control your opponent before he senses what is going on.

The disadvantages are: 1. Opportunities to apply the techniques do not occur very often. Finger Chin Na is most easily applied when your opponent's hand is open. However, while fighting or sparring most people keep their hands closed, and so the fingers are hard to reach. 2. If your opponent senses your intention before you control his finger, he can easily escape. If his hand and fingers are sweaty it is particularly difficult to control them. 3. Finger techniques are harder to learn. If your opponent would stand still and open his fingers for you to grab, it would be easy for you to control him. Unfortunately, in a real fight you do not know how your opponent will attack you, so in order for you to be effective, you must know and choose an appropriate technique, and you must be fast, smooth, and skillful. To reach this level requires a great deal of practice.

Finger Chin Na is used most often when sticking techniques are used. This is because the hands must be open while sticking in order to sense the opponent. Sticking is used most often in southern styles such as snake, crane, and dragon, and in of the internal styles such as Tai Chi and Liu Ho Ba Fa. Finger Chin Na is also commonly used when the opponent tries to grapple, since to do so he must open his fingers.

3-2. Finger Chin Na Techniques

This section will discuss finger Chin Na, breaking it down into six categories. Each category will be made up of similar techniques, so once you can understand the first technique, you will be able to understand the second with less effort. Remember that the main purpose of this book is to show you the keys and the principles of the techniques. We do not encourage step by step learning or always following exactly the same approach. You are encouraged to find new ways to approach the techniques. For example, there may be at least three ways to achieve a certain control or technique, and this book will present only one which is considered typical. Furthermore, this book may present an approach to one technique which you may find to be the best way for you to apply another technique.

In the first chapter we discussed the principles of how misplacing the bone and dividing the muscle/tendon techniques work. Before we start discussing finger Chin Na techniques, you should understand the structure of the fingers, especially the joints. A finger joint is constructed of bones, ligaments, cartilage, tendons, and muscles (Figure 3-1). You can see that there is not much muscle or tendon in the fingers. When you apply pressure or twist the joint in the wrong direction, the pain comes from the ligaments and cartilage tearing and separating, which is the characteristic of misplacing the bone techniques. Most finger Chin Na fall into this category, though there are some dividing the muscle/tendon techniques which are applied to the base of fingers where the muscles are bigger and easier to control.

We would like to point out here that there are only two angles which are effective for finger Chin Na. One is backward (Figure 3-2) and the other is sideward (Figure 3-3). In misplacing the bone techniques, the backward direction is generally more effective when you want to control the person, but when you want to actually move the bone out of joint, the sideward direction is better. Another point is that sideward control is easier to escape from than backward control. However, for dividing the muscle/tendon techniques, sideward is more effective than backward.

As mentioned before, it is usually very difficult to separate the misplacing the bone aspect from the dividing the muscle/tendon aspect,

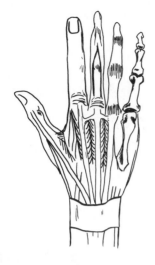

Figure 3-1.

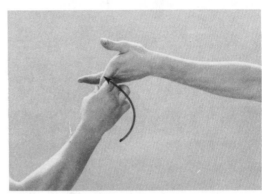

Figure 3-2.

Figure 3-3.

Figure 3-4.

because most techniques combine them. In the following techniques we will list only the major control principle. There are usually several counterattacks possible for each grabbing Chin Na, but we will list only one. Once you have mastered the techniques in this book you will soon catch the trick to how one technique can be used against another. When a general counterattack is used, it will not be discussed in detail.

A. Woh Jyy Fan (Holding Finger Turning) 握指翻

Holding finger(s) and turning is probably the most common technique which most people already know. You simply hold your opponent's finger(s) tight and turn them backwards or sidewards.

1. Dan Jyy Woh (Single Finger Holding) 單指握

Technique #1: In single finger holding, hold your opponent's finger or thumb and bend it backwards or to the side of the fingers. Figure 3-4 shows a control which bends the finger up and back, while Figure 3-5 shows downward holding control. In addition, Figure 3-6 shows

Figure 3-5.

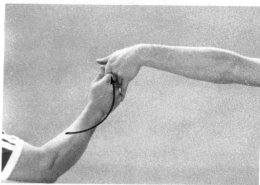

Figure 3-6.

Figure 3-7.

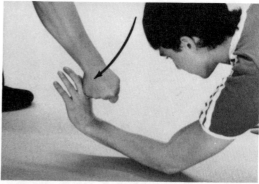

Figure 3-8.

sideward control. To prevent your opponent from kicking you or attacking your face, you should extend your arm as much as possible to keep him away. When you use a Chin Na which lifts the opponent up, you must make his heels come off the floor (Figure 3-7), otherwise he will be able to kick you. For the same reason, when you control your opponent by pressing him down, you should make his elbow or face touch the floor (Figure 3-8) or he can still react against you.

Principle: This is a misplacing the bone technique when used for upward or downward, but it also includes a dividing the muscle/tendon Chin Na when it is used to control sideways. When you use your hand to hold one of your opponent's fingers, you have two advantages. The first is that your hand is stronger than his finger. The second is that it is harder for your opponent to apply a finger Chin Na to counterattack you.

Escape and Counter: The easiest way to escape is to kick the opponent's shin or poke his eyes before he has completely controlled you, and at the same time pull back your finger. To counterattack, rotate your hand and finger and at the same time use your other hand to grab his wrist (Figure 3-9). Then twist his wrist and control him (Figure 3-10).

2. Duo Jyy Woh (Multiple Finger Holding) 多指握

Technique #2: This technique is exactly the same as Technique #1 except

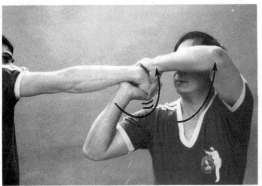

Figure 3-9.

Figure 3-10.

Figure 3-11.

Figure 3-12.

that when you apply it you grab more than one of your opponent's fingers. Generally speaking, you need more strength to control two or more fingers at the same time than you do to control one. The advantage of multiple finger control over Single Finger Holding is that it is harder for your opponent to rotate and escape. As with single finger control, multiple finger control can be upward, downward, and sideways. Again, you must be fast, keep your opponent away from you, and lift him up off his heels or press him down to the floor.

Principle: Hold two or more fingers to prevent the opponent from rotating his hand out of your control. If you bend upward or downward it is a misplacing the bone technique, but when you bend sideways it also includes dividing the muscle/tendon Chin Na.

Escape and Counter: See Technique #1.

3. Faan Bei Joan (Back Turning) 反背轉

Technique #3: The Back Turning technique is an alternative position in multiple finger control. Whenever you have a chance to grab your opponent's fingers, press his fingers down and move to his rear (Figure 3-11). Once you have moved his fingers to his back, rotate your hand to increase the pressure until his heels leave the floor (Figure 3-12). In order to prevent him from resisting or counterattacking, you can use your left

Figure 3-13.   Figure 3-14.   Figure 3-15.

hand to grab his throat. Alternatively, right after you gain control over him with your right hand, switch the control to your left hand while your right hand locks his neck (Figure 3-13).

Principle: This is a misplacing the bone technique. However, it also includes some of the dividing the muscle/tendon technique in the shoulder area. When you apply this technique, you must move your body to his side in order to circle his hand to his back and also to prevent him from punching with his other hand. If you also control his throat, you force his head upward, which will effectively prevent him from doing anything.

Escape and Counter: To escape, refer to Technique #1. To counter, while your opponent steps his left leg to your side, you also step your left leg back to face him and at the same time use your right hand to grab his right wrist (Figure 3-14). Then immediately use both of your hands to lock his right wrist upward (Figure 3-15).

B. Gieh Ya Far (Knuckle Press Method) 節壓法

The Knuckle Press Method is a little different from the above techniques. Instead of using your hand, in knuckle press control you use your thumb or finger to press down directly on your opponent's finger joint and misplace the bones.

1. Moo Jyy Ya (Thumb Press) 姆指壓

Technique #4: When you find the opportunity, for example when shaking hands (Figure 3-16), place your index finger on the opponent's first thumb joint and your thumb on the base of his thumb. Apply pressure by tilting your hand counterclockwise (Figure 3-17). The trick is to try to keep your index finger and thumb perpendicular to his thumb. In order to prevent him from kicking you or otherwise fighting back, simply step your right leg backward and bring him to the ground (Figure 3-18).

Principle: Misplacing the bone. Your thumb and second finger generate torque with rotating pressure on the base of the opponent's thumb, which may tear the cartilage and ligament off the bone.

Escape and Counter: Before the opponent has completely controlled you, kick his shin or attack his eyes to distract his attention and pull your thumb back immediately. Alternatively, you may use your other hand to hold his wrist to prevent his continuing the action, and pull your thumb

Figure 3-16.

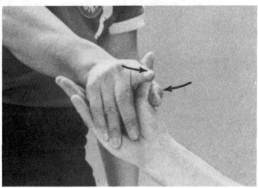

Figure 3-17.

Figure 3-18.

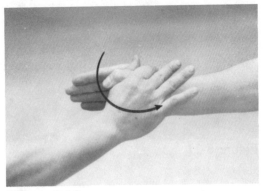

Figure 3-19.

back immediately. To counterattack, first rotate your thumb to prevent it from being controlled (Figure 3-19) and use your left hand to grab the opponent's pinky (Figure 3-20). Immediately press both his thumb and pinky downward (Figure 3-21).

2. Shiah Ya Jyy (Low Finger Press) 下壓指
Technique #5: There are two common ways of doing a low finger press. The first is to rotate to the side, which is similar to the last thumb control (Figure 3-22). The other is to rotate forward (Figure 3-23). When you rotate to the side, step your right leg backward and press his hand down to your right until his elbow touches the floor (Figure 3-24). When you rotate forward, you should also step backward while pressing him down in front of you (Figure 3-25).

Principle: Misplacing the bone. Use rotation and finger press to extend the opponent's cartilage and ligaments. This will cause the cartilage and ligament fiber to tear off or separate from the bone. When you use this technique the fingers of your controlling hand are open, so you must be

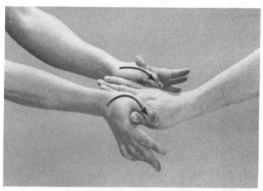

Figure 3-20.

Figure 3-21.

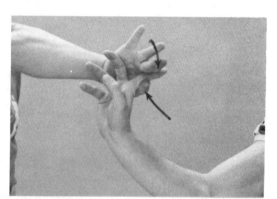

Figure 3-22.

Figure 3-23.

Figure 3-24.

Figure 3-25.

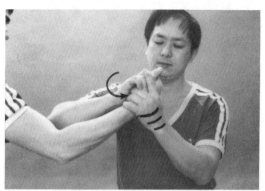

Figure 3-26.

Figure 3-27.

wary of an attempt by your opponent to apply a finger Chin Na on you.
Escape and Counter: Since your opponent has to press down to rotate your fingers, you can easily punch his face to distract his attention and pull your fingers back. To counterattack, first rotate the finger being controlled and at the same time use the other hand to grab his wrist (Figure 3-26). Then circle your elbow and lock his elbow (Figure 3-27).

C. Shang Diau Far (Upper Hook Method): 上习法

In the Upper Hook Method, you use your finger(s) to lock the opponent's finger(s) and then rotate up to raise him. Right after your lock, you must rotate quickly before your opponent rotates his finger(s) and escapes.

1. Shao Jyy Kow (Small Finger Hook) 小指扣
Technique #6: When you have a chance to use your pinky and ring finger to grab your opponent's pinky or any other finger, press your wrist forward and upward while rotating your pinky and ring fingers backward (Figure 3-28). You will be able to control him very effectively. For example, when you shake hands, first rotate your wrist to the side (Figure 3-29) and immediately press your wrist forward and upward to control him until his heels leave the floor (Figure 3-30).
Principle: Misplacing the bone. When you rotate your wrist to the side you have set up the right position for controlling him. If you press your wrist forward, you will be able to raise his body up by putting pressure on his knuckle. When you control your opponent, do not raise your elbow. To force him up, simply increase the rotation pressure on his pinky.
Escape and Counter: Once your finger is grabbed, pull your elbow in to your chest, rotate your arm, and bend your fingers in, and at the same time pull his hand away with your other hand. To counter, you can rotate your body to the right and step your left leg forward. This will stop him from further controlling you. While you are doing this, also rotate your right arm counterclockwise and use your left hand to grab his wrist while your right thumb presses his thumb (Figure 3-31).

2. Shang Fan Jyy (Upward Finger Turn) 上分指
Technique #7: There are two common ways to do this technique, both using the thumb, index, and middle fingers. The first way is to place your

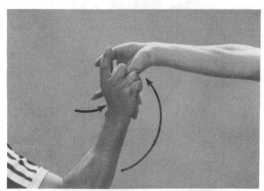

Figure 3-28.

Figure 3-29.

Figure 3-30.

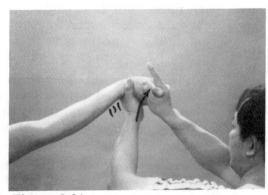

Figure 3-31.

thumb on the second joint of any of your opponent's finger's while your second and middle fingers lock his first joint (Figure 3-32). Once you have locked his finger this way, immediately rotate your wrist and force his body up until his heels leave the floor (Figure 3-33). The second way to do this technique is to grab his finger the same way, but with your thumb and fingers the reverse of the way shown above (Figure 3-34). Raise him up so his heels are off the ground (Figure 3-35).

Principle: Misplacing the bone. Your thumb and index finger create a torque which can easily control the opponent's finger joint.

Escape and Counter: Since your opponent does not actually grab you, you can easily pull back and escape before you are locked into the position. To counter, you can rotate your left hand and at the same time use the other hand to grab his right hand (Figure 3-36). Then turn his palm to face you and use both hands to control his thumb and pinky (Figure 3-37).

Figure 3-32.

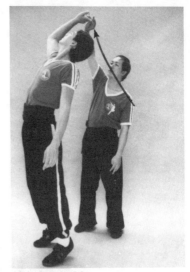

Figure 3-33.

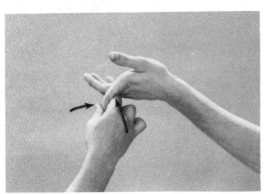

Figure 3-34.

Figure 3-35.

Figure 3-36.

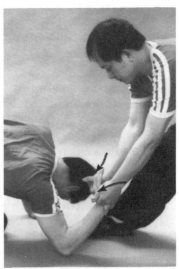

Figure 3-37.

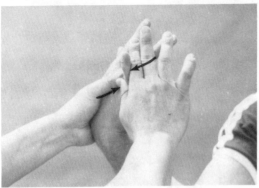

Figure 3-38.

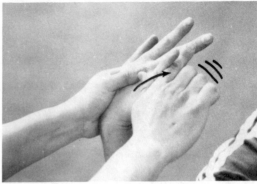

Figure 3-39.

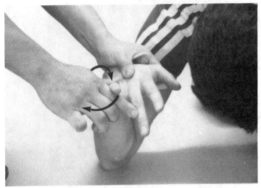

Figure 3-40.

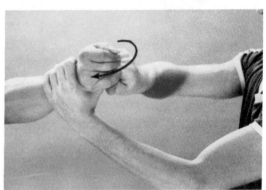

Figure 3-41.

D. Joan Sou Far (Turning Lock Method) 轉手法
1. Joan Fen Jyy (Turning Finger Dividing) 轉分指
Technique #8: Double finger dividing uses your middle and ring fingers to grab one of the opponent's fingers, while your thumb and second finger lock another one of his fingers into position. To apply this technique, first grab any one of your opponent's fingers except the thumb with your thumb and second finger (Figure 3-38). (In this case the right hand does the Chin Na while the left hand holds the opponent's hand steady). Then grab an adjacent finger with your middle and ring fingers, and twist your hand to cross his fingers while you press your thumb forward (Figure 3-39). Press him down to the floor for your own safety (Figure 3-40).

Principle: Dividing the muscle/tendon. In this technique you twist to divide the muscle/tendon at the base of the opponent's fingers and cause pain. If you also increase the pressure from your thumb to his joint, you can increase his pain through misplacing the bone.

Escape and Counter: When your finger is grabbed by the opponent's thumb and index finger, immediately rotate the finger which is being grabbed to release the lock (Figure 3-41). To counterattack, right after you rotate your finger out of his control, raise your elbow and use the other hand to grab his left wrist (Figure 3-42), then press his wrist down to control him (Figure 3-43).

2. Kow Joan Gieh (Lock and Turn the Joint) 扣轉節
Technique #9: This is a finger control which will work on the opponent even if he has closed his hand into a fist. You may apply this technique on the opponent's thumb or pinky. To do this technique, use one hand to

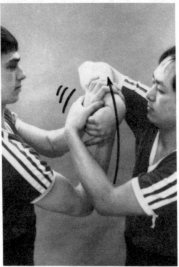

Figure 3-42.

Figure 3-43.

Figure 3-44.

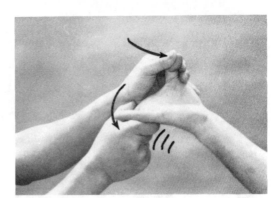

Figure 3-45.

hold his wrist, while the other hand grabs his pinky (Figure 3-44) or thumb (Figure 3-45) and twists it to the side.

Principle: Dividing the muscle/tendon and misplacing the bone. Simply twisting the joint to the side will stretch the muscles and ligaments and cause pain. In order to apply this technique, your opponent's finger must be bent first, otherwise you will not be able to lock his finger in place.

Escape and Counter: If your opponent does not hold your wrist firmly, you can easily pull back your fist. However, if he has grabbed your fist you may have to use wrist Chin Na on him in order to release the grab. Alternatively, you may use your other hand to push away the hand which is trying to control your finger, or even use a finger Chin Na on him.

3.Shao Jyy Ban (Small Finger Turning) 小指扳

Technique #10: Whenever you have a chance to grab the base of the pinky, you can simple rotate your hand and put pressure on his pinky (Figure 3-46). Remember either to make his heels leave the floor by locking his hand behind him (Figure 3-47) or force him to the floor with the help of your left hand by pushing forward against his elbow to increase the pressure (Figure 3-48). When you apply this technique, you must step to the side to prevent his punching with the other hand.

Principle: Dividing the muscle.

Escape and Counter: Before your hand is completely controlled, pull it

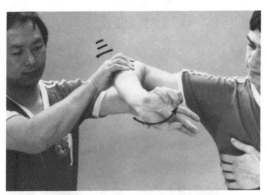

Figure 3-46.

Figure 3-47.

Figure 3-48.

Figure 3-49.

Figure 3-50.

back quickly. Alternatively, you can use the other hand to grab the fingers of his left hand and apply finger Chin Na on him.

E. Fen Cha Far (Dividing Method) 分叉法

Dividing method is a technique to divide the muscles or to tear the muscles apart and consequently cause pain. Basically, whenever you have a chance you can simply grab any two of your opponent's fingers with your two hands and split them apart.

1. Shang Diau Fen (Upper Hook Dividing) 上刁分

Technique #11: In this technique, first use one hand to grab the opponent's last two fingers and pull them to the side (Figure 3-49). Immediately use your other hand to pull his elbow into the inside of your elbow (Figure 3-50). Then raise your hand and pull and rotate your wrist downward to cause his muscles to split (Figures 3-51 and 3-52). You should use your index finger to set his hand in the right angle for control. Raise his heels off the floor and keep your body to his side to prevent him from attacking you with the other hand.

Figure 3-51.

Figure 3-52.

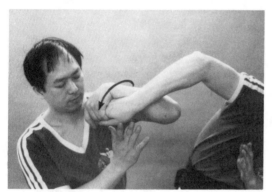

Figure 3-53.

Figure 3-54.

Principle: Dividing the muscle. Remember to use the second finger to direct the angle of control.

Escape and Counter: Once you have sensed that your fingers have been grabbed, you should rotate your wrist and close your fingers, and at the same time pull your elbow in and use the other hand to push away the hand which is grabbing you. Alternatively, since your opponent has to approach you to apply this technique, you may just use the other hand to punch his face and at the same time pull your hand back. To counter, once you have sensed the opponent's grab, pull your hand in (Figure 3-53) and use your right hand to lock his thumb (Figure 3-54).

2. Shiah Diau Fen (Lower Hook Dividing) 下刁分

Technique #12: First grab the opponent's last two fingers as in technique #11 and pull his arm down to keep it straight (Figure 3-55). Immediately cross your elbow above his elbow (Figure 3-56) and bend your right knee down while pulling your right hand up and pressing your right shoulder down (Figure 3-57). You should also use your left hand to push the opponent's hand up to cause pain in his wrist (Figure 3-58). This will bring him to his knees on the floor.

Principle: Dividing the muscle. This technique is a mixture of finger and wrist Chin Na. The finger control separates the muscles while the wrist control twists the muscles.

Escape and Counter: Refer to Technique #11.

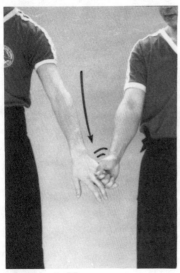

Figure 3-55.　　　　Figure 3-56.　　　　Figure 3-57.

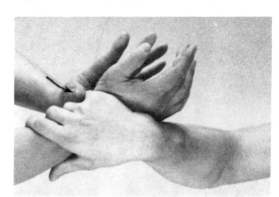

Figure 3-58.　　　　　　　Figure 3-59.

3. Shao Charn Jyy (Small Wrap Finger) 小纏指

Technique #13: When your opponent's right hand touches your right wrist or forearm, use your left hand to cover his pinky and lock it in place (Figure 3-59). Then rotate your right arm to the side and press down while your left hand, which is still holding his pinky, pushes it to the side (Figure 3-60). You should press him down until his body nears the floor.

Principle: Dividing the muscle. This is a very quick and effective technique to use whenever your opponent touches your wrist or arm with his fingers. This technique is similar to the wrist Chin Na called Small Wrap Hand. The difference is that this technique controls a finger while the other controls the wrist. This means that when you control your opponent, the pain is generated from his finger instead of his wrist.

Escape and Counter: Pull your hand back before it is locked in place. Use your other hand to push his left hand away to prevent him from locking your pinky. Distracting his attention can also be effective. Either a finger or a wrist Chin Na can be applied to counter this technique.

4. Shuang Fen Jyy (Double Fingers Split) 伙分指

Technique #14: In this technique you simply use your two hands to grab any two groups of your opponent's fingers and split them apart (Figure 3-61).

Principle: Dividing the muscle.

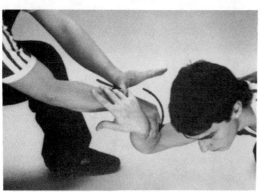

Figure 3-60.

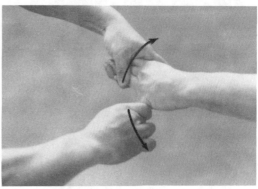

Figure 3-61.

Figure 3-62.

Figure 3-63.

Escape and Counter: Since your opponent has to use both hands to grab your fingers, you can simply use your other hand to punch him or use your leg to kick him, and immediately pull your grabbed hand back.

F. Jin Shou Far (Lock Tightly Method) 緊鎖法

The lock tightly method is an effective way to control an opponent and take him with you. Policemen can use it to control criminals without using handcuffs.

1. Kow Long Tao (Control the Dragon's Head) 扣龍頭

Technique #15: If your opponent grabs your right wrist with his right hand (Figure 3-62), bend your elbow and pull your hand in, and at the same time use your left hand to pull his thumb and forearm together (Figures 3-63 and 3-64). If instead your opponent uses his left hand to grab your right wrist (Figure 3-65), sink your elbow and coil your hand above his wrist, and at the same time use your left hand to hold his thumb and forearm together (Figures 3-66 and 3-67).

Principle: Dividing the muscle.

Escape and Counter: Before you are completely controlled, you must use your other hand to stop your opponent from controlling your thumb and forearm. Alternatively, you can use your other hand to punch him or use a leg to kick him and at the same time pull your hand back.

Figure 3-64.

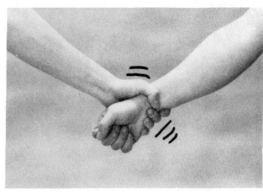

Figure 3-65.

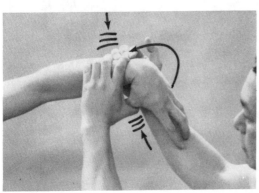

Figure 3-66.

Figure 3-67.

2. Kow Long Wei (Control the Dragon's Tail) 扣龍尾
Technique #16: This technique is very similar to Technique #15 except that the pinky is controlled instead of the thumb (Figure 3-68).
Principle: Misplacing the bone. Notice that the principle used in this technique is different from that of technique #15.
Escape and Counter: Refer to Technique #15.

3. Shang Diau Jyy (Up Hook Finger) 上刁指
Technique #17: This technique is very similar to Technique #11. The only difference is that you pull your opponent's finger(s) down and back to misplace the bones instead of divide the muscle/tendon (Figures 3-69 and 3-70).
Principle: Misplacing the bone.
Escape and Counter: Refer to Technique #11.

Figure 3-68.

Figure 3-69.

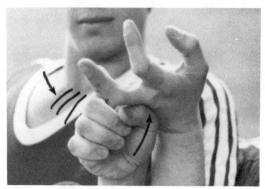

Figure 3-70.

CHAPTER 4

WRIST CHIN NA

4-1. Introduction

You will usually need to use more power for a wrist Chin Na than for a finger Chin Na, simply because the wrist is stronger than the fingers. However, you still should not need to use more than one-half of the strength of your opponent—if you need more strength than this your technique is probably wrong. Chinese Chin Na uses a great many wrist Chin Na techniques. This is because the wrist is usually easy to reach, and once a wrist Chin Na is applied, it is very hard to escape from. Very often a finger Chin Na is used at the same time to double the control of the opponent. When a wrist Chin Na is used together with a finger Chin Na, it is called Small Circle (Shao Jiuan). However, when a wrist Chin Na is used together with an elbow control, it is called Medium Circle (Jong Jiuan).

Before you learn wrist Chin Na, you should study the structure of the wrist so that you will know how wrist Chin Na works. The wrist is made up of eight bones, which are held together with and covered by ligaments (Figure 4-1). Passing over the bones and ligaments are many different tendons which connect the muscles of the arm and hand. Then there is a retinaculum which surrounds and covers the ligaments and tendons of the wrist to enhance the strength of the wrist (Figure 4-2). Because of the way the wrist is constructed, it is very hard to use misplacing the bone Chin Na. However, dividing the muscle/tendon techniques can work very well. Since the wrist area is covered with many tendons, ligaments, and the retinaculum, any time you bend or twist it to an abnormal angle you can easily tear the fibers and cause pain.

For generations teachers have passed down four words to help students catch the keys to wrist Chin Na—wrap, press, twist, and bend. Once you learn the techniques right, you will find you need little strength to apply wrist Chin Na. If you do not catch the tricks, you will need to use a lot of power, and you will also be in danger of your opponent escaping and counterattacking. These four key words are usually trained by watching first, then feeling and experiencing, and then by accumulating experience. If you can grasp these tricks, you can say that you have learned the keys to

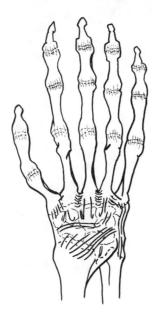

Figure 4-1.

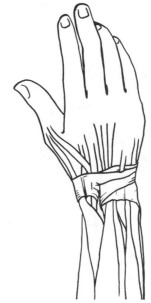

Figure 4-2.

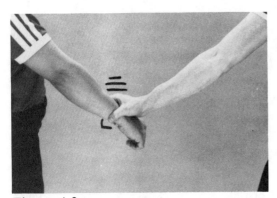

Figure 4-3.

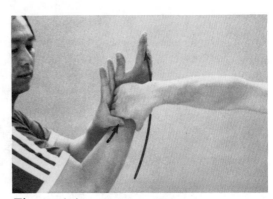

Figure 4-4.

wrist Chin Na control. All of the following techniques are mixtures of these key words.

4-2. Wrist Chin Na Techniques
A. Charn Far (Wrapping Method) 纏法
1. Shao Charn Sou-1 (Small Wrap Hand-1) 小纏手 - 1

Technique #18: This technique is very common and is trained in almost every Chinese martial style, although there are slight differences in applications. We will show here the technique as done by the crane style, which the author considers to be the most effective. When someone grabs your right wrist or right forearm with his right hand (Figure 4-3), cover his hand with your left hand, making sure to **LOCK HIS INDEX FINGER WITH YOUR THUMB** (Figure 4-4). This lock will prevent him from opening his hand and escaping. At the same time turn your right palm to face you. Then turn your hand forward and wrap it over his wrist and push downward **WITH YOUR FINGERS POINTING DOWNWARD** (Figure 4-5). This is a form of crane wing dropping as trained by the crane style. Remember **DO NOT PUSH YOUR HAND TO YOUR RIGHT**. You will lose the correct angle so that you are

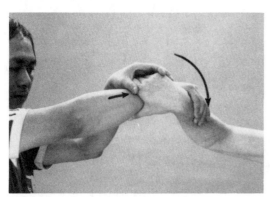

Figure 4-5.

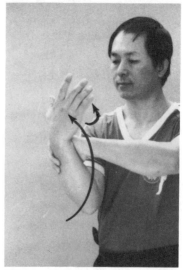

Figure 4-6.

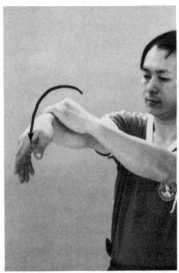

Figure 4-7.

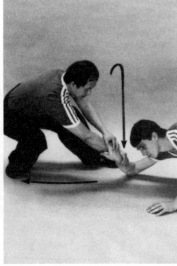

Figure 4-8.

Figure 4-9.

controlling the wrong muscles, and your opponent will be able to turn and hit you with his elbow. In training, turn both of your hands upward with the palms facing you (Figure 4-6) and then turn outward and finally downward, forming wings (Figure 4-7). When you control his wrist, you must also step your right leg backward to set up for a kick in case your control fails. For a complete control, **YOU MUST PRESS YOUR HAND DOWN UNTIL HIS ELBOW TOUCHES THE FLOOR** (Figure 4-8), otherwise he will still be able to resist and counterattack. Remember, if you do this technique right, **YOUR ENEMY WILL NOT BE ABLE TO TURN AROUND AND HIT YOU WITH HIS ELBOW (Figure 4-9) OR PUNCH YOU WITH HIS LEFT HAND** (Figure 4-10).

Principle: Dividing the muscle/tendon. In this technique, you first wrap your opponent's hand and wrist to prevent him from escaping. Then you rotate to the correct angle to twist his wrist muscles and tendons, and finally press down with your fingers pointing downward to bend his muscles and tendons and control him completely.

Escape and Counter: In order to prevent your opponent from wrapping

Figure 4-10.

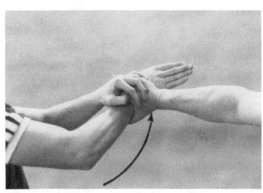

Figure 4-11.

Figure 4-12.

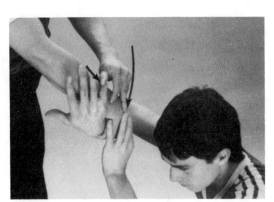

Figure 4-13.

his hand around your wrist, simply push his grabbing hand to your right (Figure 4-11). This will stop him from wrapping further. There are at least five ways to counterattack against this technique. Here we will demonstrate the easiest and best way. When your opponent has wrapped his hand around your wrist, use your left hand to lock his pinky and push it to the side (Figure 4-12), and at the same time put pressure on his wrist with your right hand (Figure 4-13)(refer to Technique #13: Small Wrap Finger).

2. Shao Charn Sou-2 (Small Wrap Hand-2) 小纏手 - 2

Technique #19: This technique is very similar to the last one and controls the same group of muscles with the same controlling angle. The difference in this technique is that you use it when your opponent uses his left hand to grab your right wrist (Figure 4-14). When this happens, cover his hand with your left hand and use your thumb to lock his index finger (Figure 4-15). Then wrap your right hand from the outside of his hand and press down the same way as in Technique #18 (Figures 4-16 and 4-17). Remember: do not push to the side and allow your opponent to turn and attack you; make sure you bring him down until his elbow touches the floor; and step your right leg back so you will be prepared for a killing kick if necessary.

Principle: Dividing the muscle/tendon. Refer to Technique #18.

Figure 4-14.

Figure 4-15.

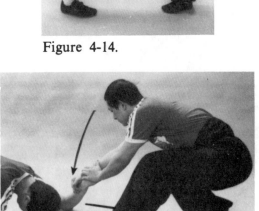

Figure 4-16.

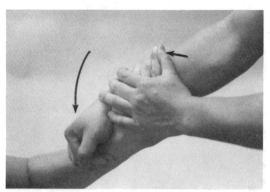

Figure 4-17.

Escape and Counter: As with Technique #18, you can push your hand to the side to prevent his hand from wrapping yours. To counter, you can use the same technique as with Technique #18. Alternatively, you may use your other hand to grab one of the fingers of his right hand as he attempts to wrap your arm (Figure 4-18), and bend it backward and down, controlling his arm with your left hand so that he cannot twist out of your grip (Figure 4-19)(refer to Technique #5: Low Finger Press).

3. Da Charn Sou (Large Wrap Hand) 大纏手

Technique #20: Large wrap hand uses the same principle as the last two techniques, but the way you wrap is different. When someone grabs your right wrist with his right hand (Figure 4-20), step your left leg forward as you raise your right hand in front of you, and at the same time move your left hand under his forearm to cover and wrap his right hand (Figure 4-21). Lock his right elbow with your left elbow to prevent him from elbowing you. As your left hand is wrapping his hand, raise the fingers of your right hand and then press down on his forearm with the same trick used in the last two techniques (Figures 4-22 and 4-23). You should bow forward and press down until his left hand touches the floor, otherwise he can still punch your face with it. Make sure to use the correct angle on his wrist or he can turn and use his left elbow to strike you. If you find you have failed to control him, you can kick him with your right leg. If he

Figure 4-18.

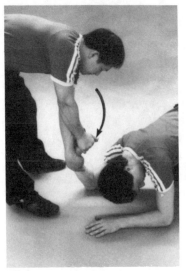

Figure 4-19.

Figure 4-20.

Figure 4-21.

Figure 4-22.

starts to turn around with the intention of striking you with his left elbow, you can also change your technique to the next one which will allow you to control him again.

Principle: Dividing the muscle/tendon. This technique is commonly used in close range fighting. It is fast and your opponent will usually not sense your attempt as easily as the last two techniques.

Escape and Counter: Whenever your hand is wrapped in this technique, it is pretty hard for you to pull it out. Fortunately, since you are close to your opponent, you can easily use your left hand to strike his face to force him to release your hand. To counter against this technique you may use your left hand to cover his left hand (Figure 4-24) and twist his wrist to control it (Figure 4-25).

4. Faan Charn Sou (Back Wrap Hand) 反缠手

Technique #21: The same muscles are controlled by this technique as by the previous three, only now the wrist is controlled by lifting instead of pressing down. When your opponent grabs your right wrist with his right

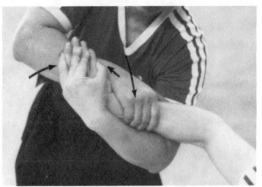

Figure 4-23.

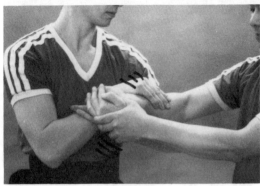

Figure 4-24.

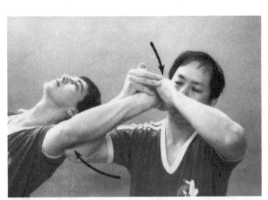

Figure 4-25.

Figure 4-26.

hand (Figure 4-26), step your left leg to his right side as you circle your right hand clockwise to weaken his grip (Figure 4-27). Your right hand grasps the side of his wrist as your left hand grasps his hand. Your palm is on the back of his hand, with your fingers grasping the edge of his hand. Your left hand twists his wrist clockwise and bends the hand away from you, and your right hand pushes upward (Figure 4-28). As you are doing this, you should also step your right leg behind him (Figure 4-29). Control the opponent by lifting up with both hands. Remember that **YOU MUST LIFT HIM UP UNTIL HIS HEELS LEAVE THE FLOOR, OTHERWISE HE IS NOT COMPLETELY CONTROLLED AND CAN KICK YOU.**

Principle: Dividing the muscle/tendon. This technique can cause extreme pain. If you want to cause more pain, grab his pinky with your left hand instead of his palm (Figure 4-30).

Escape and Counter: Your first reaction against this technique is to pull your elbow in and punch his face with your left hand. To counterattack, when your opponent wraps his right hand around your wrist, grab the fingers of his right hand with your left hand (Figure 4-31) and press him down (Figure 4-32).

Figure 4-27.

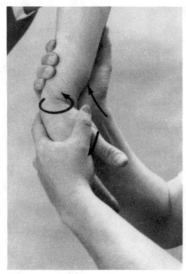

Figure 4-28.

Figure 4-29.

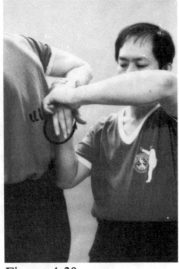

Figure 4-30.

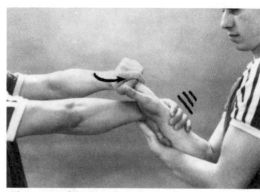

Figure 4-31.

B. Ya Wan (Wrist Press) 壓腕
1. Chyan Ya Wan (Forward Wrist Press) 前壓腕

Technique #22: Forward press is a very common wrist Chin Na, and different approaches can lead to different techniques. Whenever you have a chance to grab the opponent's hand, quickly grasp his forearm with your other hand to prevent him from escaping, and immediately squeeze your two hands together (Figure 4-33). This will cause extreme pain and control him easily. When you apply this technique, press him down until his knee touches the floor and move your body to his side to keep away from his other hand and possible counterattacks (Figure 4-34).

Principle: Dividing the muscle/tendon. Pressing his hand against his forearm will overextend his ligaments and tendons, tearing the fibers and causing intense pain. However, sometimes you may encounter a person who has stretched a great deal and can easily touch his fingers to his arm. Against such a person a wrist press is useless. If you have applied a wrist press on someone and suddenly find it isn't working, punch his face or switch to a finger or elbow control.

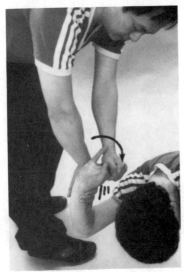

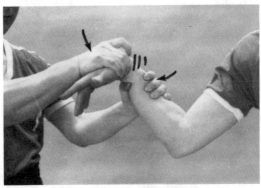

Figure 4-33.

Figure 4-32.

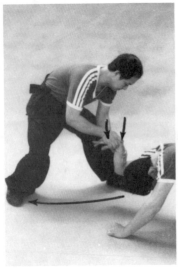

Figure 4-35.

Figure 4-34.

Escape and Counter: When your hand is grabbed, your first reaction should be to tense your wrist and arm and try to close your fingers as soon as possible. You can then use the other hand to grab either of his hands to apply a Chin Na on him. One of the common counters is to use your left hand to grab his right hand (Figure 4-35), twist and bend to control his wrist (Figure 4-36).

2. Shang Ya Wan (Press the Wrist up) 上壓腕

Technique #23: This technique is similar to Technique #22, but the approach and the control are different. In this technique, once you have grabbed the opponent's right hand, grasp his right elbow with your left hand (Figure 4-37). Lift his elbow upward as you press his hand·forward and then up (Figure 4-38). You must apply enough pressure to make his heels leave the floor. To enhance the pain, you can squeeze your left hand down while you press your right hand up. Also, as you apply the technique you should move to his side so that you are protected from his left hand.

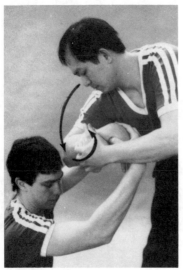

Figure 4-36.

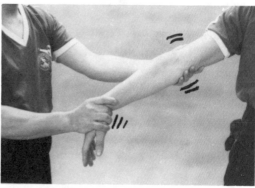

Figure 4-37.

Figure 4-38.

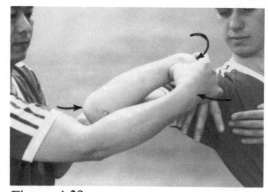

Figure 4-39.

Principle: Dividing the muscle/tendon. Refer to Technique #22.
Escape and Counter: When your hand is grabbed, your first reaction should be to tense your wrist and arm and to try to close your fingers as soon as possible. You can then use your other hand to grab either of his hands to apply a Chin Na on him. You may use Technique #18: Small Wrap Hand for your counterattack.

3. Shiah Ney Ya Wan (Low Inward Wrist Press) 下內壓腕
Technique #24: This technique is also similar to Technique #22, with a different approach and control. Once you have grabbed the opponent's right hand, you again grasp his right elbow with your left hand. Pull your left hand toward you while your right hand presses his hand toward his elbow and bends his hand toward him (Figure 4-39). You must apply enough pressure and bow forward so that his left hand touches the ground, otherwise his can still resist you (Figure 4-40).
Principle: Dividing the muscle/tendon. Refer to Technique #22.
Escape and Counter: Refer to Technique #23.

Figure 4-40.

Figure 4-41.

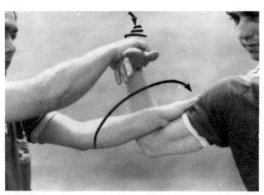

Figure 4-42.

Figure 4-43.

4. Shiah Way Ya Wan (Low Outward Wrist Press) 下外壓腕

Technique #25: This technique is also similar to Technique #22, with a different approach and control. Once you have grabbed the opponent's right hand, press his elbow to your right with your left arm (Figure 4-41). Coil your left hand around his forearm until you reach his elbow (Figure 4-42), then push his elbow down while your right hand presses his hand downward (Figure 4-43). When you control, keep his forearm perpendicular to the floor and push him down until his elbow touches the floor. Step your right leg back in case you need to kick.

Principle: Dividing the muscle/tendon. Refer to Technique #22.

Escape and Counter: Refer to Technique #23.

5. Faan Ya Wan (Reverse Wrist Press) 反壓腕

Technique #26: This technique is a counterattack against a wrist grab. Whenever your opponent has grabbed your right wrist with his right hand for any reason (Figure 4-44), simply rotate your right arm counterclockwise and grab his wrist with your left hand, with your thumb

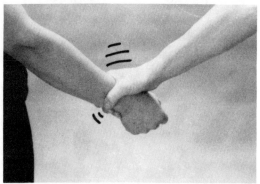

Figure 4-44.

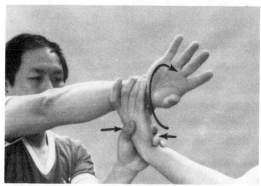

Figure 4-45.

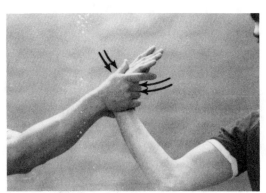

Figure 4-46.

Figure 4-47.

pressing the base of his pinky (Figure 4-45). Press your thumb forward and pull your right hand free, then hold his hand with both of your hands and push forward and downward while your right leg steps backward (Figures 4-46 and 4-47). You must press him down until his elbow touches the floor for a complete control.

Principle: Dividing the muscle/tendon. Refer to Technique #22.

Escape and Counter: Once you have found that your wrist grab is stopped, pull your hand back as soon as possible to escape from your opponent's countergrabbing. However, if you are too late and your hand is already grabbed, use your left hand to lock his right pinky and press him down (Figure 4-48).

6. Bah Wang Chiing Keh (Feudal Lord Invites to Dinner) 霸王請客
Technique #27: This technique is commonly used by policemen to control prisoners without the use of handcuffs. Pull your opponent's right wrist with your right hand as your left shoulder and upper arm press his elbow forward to keep it straight (Figure 4-49). Immediately use your left forearm to lock his arm (Figure 4-50), push your right hand toward his face, and use both hands to press his hand down toward his forearm (Figure 4-51). Remember to stay on his side so that you are safe from his other hand. Inflict enough pain so that his heels leave the floor. If he

Figure 4-48.

Figure 4-49.

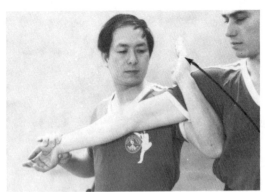

Figure 4-50.

Figure 4-51.

attempts to resist or counterattack, just squeeze more. If you encounter an opponent who is double jointed, you may not be able to control his wrist this way. In such a case, use your right hand to control his pinky for complete control (Figure 4-52).

Principle: Dividing the muscle/tendon, though if you are also controlling his pinky finger then you are also using misplacing the bone. Remember that you will often use several techniques at the same time in order to control him effectively.

Escape and Counter: Once you sense your opponent's grab, immediately pull your elbow into your chest to prevent him from controlling it. Be alert, because he may punch as you pull your arm back. To counter, you can grab his left wrist with your left hand and push it toward him (Figure 4-53). Then grab his right wrist with your right hand and pull it to your right so that his arms are crossed (Figure 4-54). Finally, press his right hand down while your left hand controls his left wrist (Figure 4-55).

7. Yee Ji Jaan Chyh (Wild Chicken Spreads Its Wings) 野雞展翅
Technique #28: Step your right foot to your opponent's right side as you grab his right hand with your right hand (Figure 4-56). Turn your body to your right as you step your left leg behind him and grab his wrist with your left hand (Figure 4-57), and finally press him down with the base of

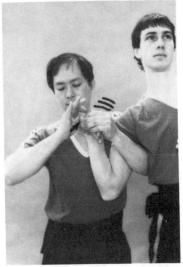

Figure 4-52.

Figure 4-53.

Figure 4-54.

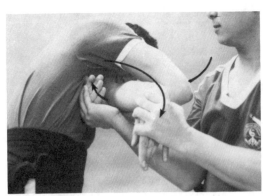

Figure 4-55.

Figure 4-56.

Figure 4-57.

Figure 4-58.

both thumbs (Figure 4-58). Remember to press with the base of your thumbs and not the tips, and to force him down until his face touches the floor.

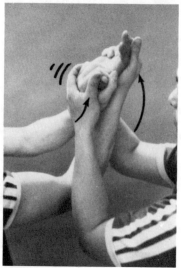

Figure 4-59.

Figure 4-60.

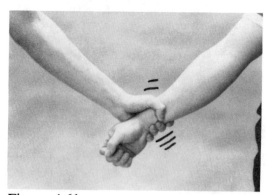

Figure 4-61.

Figure 4-62.

Principle: Dividing the muscle/tendon. This is a large circle Chin Na since you must take two steps to complete the control. You may add a finger Chin Na if you need to or wish to.

Escape and Counter: Because this is a large circle Chin Na, it can be sensed easily. Once you sense the grab, simply pull your hand back immediately. You can also stop the control by stepping back as the opponent is stepping forward. To counter, turn your body to the right and sink your elbow, and cover his right hand with your left hand (Figure 4-59). Finally, use both hands to control his wrist (Figure 4-60).

C. Joan Wan (Turning Wrist) 轉腕

1. Shuenn Shoei Tuei Jou (Push the Boat to Follow the Stream) 順水推舟
Technique #29: This technique is commonly used against a wrist grab. When your opponent grabs your right wrist with his left hand (Figure 4-61), cover his hand with your left hand as you raise your right hand to loosen his grip (Figure 4-62). Coil your right hand to the outside of his wrist, then twist his wrist with your left hand as your right hand pushes to your left (Figure 4-63). As you are doing this, turn and lower your body to the position shown to prevent your opponent from turning his body and escaping (Figure 4-64). When you lower your body, it is the turning of your body which generates the power to push his arm to the side. Sometimes you may find an opponent whose wrists are very strong or

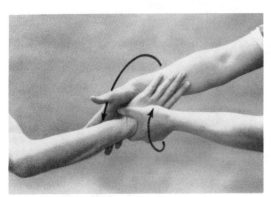

Figure 4-63.

Figure 4-64.

Figure 4-65.

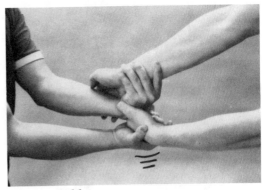

Figure 4-66.

who stiffens his wrists to make your control difficult. This may be overcome by adding a finger Chin Na to the technique (Figure 4-65).

Principle: Dividing the muscle/tendon. You simply twist the opponent's wrist and bend. This can tear his tendons and muscles and cause intense pain. If you add a finger Chin Na, you are also doing a misplacing the bone technique.

Escape and Counter: Since your opponent has to use both hands to control one of yours, you can easily use your other hand to punch him. This will stop the technique because he will have to withdraw his left hand to block. To counter with grabbing Chin Na, you can use your right hand to grab his left wrist (Figure 4-66) and twist it up (Figure 4-67), then turn your body 180 degrees to the right (Figure 4-68), and finally press him down to the floor (Figure 4-69). Alternatively, you can use your right hand to control fingers on his right hand (Figure 4-70) and press him down (Figure 4-71).

Figure 4-67.

Figure 4-68.

Figure 4-69.

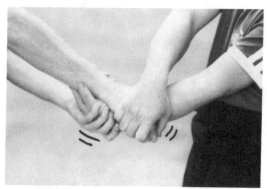

Figure 4-70.

2. Shuh Bu Torng Shyng (Forgive Me for not Going with You) 恕不同行
Technique #30: This is also a technique which can be used against a wrist grab. When your opponent grabs your right hand with his left hand (Figure 4-72), cover his hand with your left hand, hold it tight, and raise your elbow and roll over his arm (Figure 4-73). Remember to place your thumb against his index finger to prevent him from opening his hand and escaping. Finally, step back with your left foot and press him down with your elbow while holding his wrist locked in place (Figure 4-74). Force his other elbow to touch the ground to complete the control.
Principle: Dividing the muscle/tendon. The controlling principle, the muscles controlled, and the angle of pressure are the same as with wrapping Chin Na techniques. The only difference is that you press with your elbow instead of wrapping.
Escape and Counter: The best way to stop your opponent is to bend your elbow so that he cannot control it with his elbow. In addition, since he needs two hands to apply the technique, you can use your other hand to attack him and force him to withdraw his left hand to block your punch.

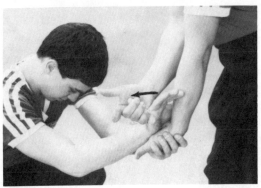

Figure 4-71.

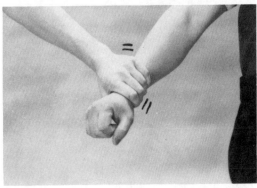

Figure 4-72.

Figure 4-73.

Figure 4-74.

To counter, you can grab his right hand with your right hand while bending your elbow (Figure 4-75), and then press him down (Figure 4-76).

3. Song For Shang Tian (Send the Buddha to Heaven) 送佛上天
Technique #31: This is a large circle Chin Na. When your opponent grabs your right wrist with his right hand, cover and grab his wrist with your left hand and swing your arms up as you step your left leg to his right side (Figure 4-77). Then step your right leg past him as you turn your body, holding his wrist tight and twisting his hand (Figure 4-78). Finally, turn to your left and step your left leg behind him while twisting and bending his wrist upward to force his heels off the floor (Figure 4-79). Remember not to turn your body in front of him, or he will be able to press his arm down and put you in an awkward position.
Principle: Dividing the muscle/tendon. This is a large circle Chin Na. It is often difficult to do this technique because of the large movement which allows your opponent to sense your intention. Speed is the key to success with this technique.
Escape and Counter: Once you sense your opponent's intention, simply pull your elbow in or step forward to bounce him off balance. This will stop him immediately. Alternatively, while he is turning his body to your

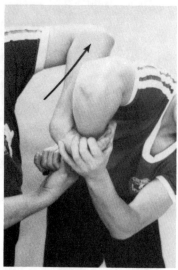
Figure 4-75.

Figure 4-76.

Figure 4-77.

Figure 4-78.

Figure 4-79.

Figure 4-80.

right, simply step forward with your left foot so that he is turning in front of you. This allows you to press your arm down and put him in an awkward position. To counter, while he is turning you can step your left leg to your left to neutralize his stepping and at the same time use your left hand to lock his left hand (Figure 4-80). Immediately twist and bend his wrist to force him to the floor (Figure 4-81).

4. Neou Joan Chyan Kuen (Turning Around Heaven and Earth) 扭轉乾坤
Technique #32: This technique can be used either as an attack or as a counterattack against a wrist grab. When your opponent grabs your right wrist with his right hand (Figure 4-82), move your hand to your right and at the same time grab his hand with your left hand (Figure 4-83). Twist your left hand counterclockwise and pull your right hand free, then use both hands to twist his wrist to the side and bend it forward as you step backward to pull him off balance (Figure 4-84). To control him effectively you must bring his elbow to the floor.
Principle: Dividing the muscle/tendon. While applying this technique

Figure 4-81.

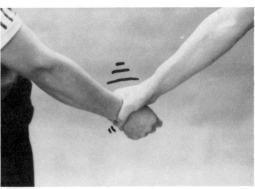

Figure 4-82.

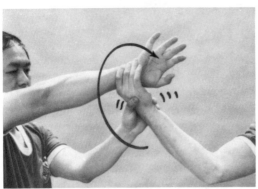

Figure 4-83.

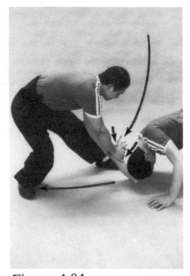

Figure 4-84.

you should step backward to pull him off balance, otherwise he will still be able to punch you with the other hand.

Escape and Counter: Use your left hand to grab his left hand and push it away. To counter, when he is turning his right hand, use your left hand to lock his pinky and control him (Figure 4-85). Alternatively, you can use your left hand to lock his left thumb (Figure 4-86) and press him down (Figure 4-87).

5. Torng Tzu Bai For (The Child Worships the Buddha) 童子拜佛
Technique #33: This technique is used when your opponent grabs the front of your shirt (Figure 4-88). Grab his hand with both hands and turn it to a control angle (Figure 4-89). The angle of control is the same as with the small wrap hand (Technique #18). If your opponent can turn his body, then your controlling angle is wrong. Then simply bend forward while holding tightly with both hands (Figure 4-90). If you find his grip is tight and his wrist is strong, you may kick him first to attract his attention to his knee, and then use the technique.

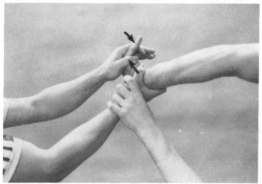

Figure 4-85.

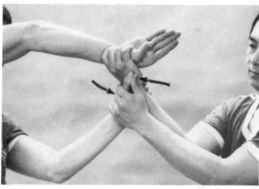

Figure 4-86.

Figure 4-87.

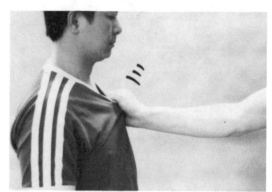

Figure 4-88.

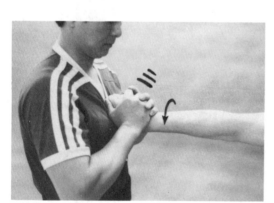

Figure 4-89.

Figure 4-90.

Principle: Dividing the muscle/tendon. Twist and bend the wrist to tear the muscle. Sometimes, however, you may find that it is easier to use a finger Chin Na.

Escape and Counter: It is not wise to hold someone's chest like this. To avoid being controlled you should pull your hand back as soon as possible. To counter, simply push his right elbow up (Figure 4-91) and then to your right as you knee him in the groin (Figure 4-92).

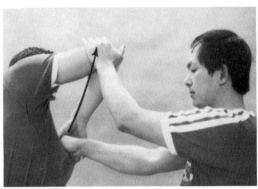

Figure 4-91.

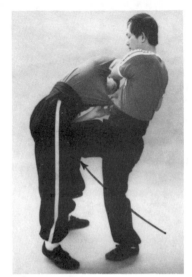

Figure 4-92.

Figure 4-93.

Figure 4-94.

6. Yee Ji Ao Chyh (Wild Chicken Breaks Its Wings) 野雞拗翅

Technique #34: This technique can also be used to counterattack when someone grabs your chest, or against a punch. This technique is very similar to Technique #33, except that this time you use your left hand to press the opponent's elbow down and lock his arm. If your opponent uses his right hand to punch, intercept and grab his hand with your right hand (Figure 4-93), then rotate his wrist to a control angle while your left hand on his elbow keeps his arm bent (Figure 4-94). Then twist his hand and bend the wrist down while pressing his elbow downward (Figure 4-95). You must apply enough pressure so that his left hand touches the floor for a complete control.

Principle: Dividing the muscle/tendon. When you twist the opponent's wrist, if you keep his elbow bent and press down on it you can increase the pain of the control and make the Chin Na more effective.

Escape and Counter: If your hand has been grabbed already, use your other hand to push his hand away while pulling your right hand back. To counter, first release the pressure on your elbow by pulling his left hand across his body with your left hand (Figure 4-96), then rotate your right hand to grab his right hand (Figure 4-97), and finally cross his arm and lock him (Figure 4-98).

Figure 4-95.

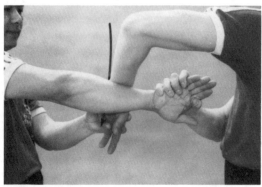

Figure 4-96.

Figure 4-97.

Figure 4-98.

7. Fan Shen Chin Yuan (Turn the Body to Seize the Monkey) 翻身擒猿

Technique #35: This technique is used against someone who grabs your shoulder from the rear. If he uses his right hand on your right shoulder, cover his hand tightly with your left hand (Figure 4-99), then turn your body to your right and at the same time raise your elbow on top of his forearm (Figures 4-100 and 4-101). Lower your body by bending your knees (Figure 4-102). To complete the control, bring him down so that his left hand touches the floor.

Principle: Dividing the muscle/tendon in the wrist and misplacing the bone in the elbow. This technique is used for a temporary control. Because it is very hard to hold your opponent's hand on your shoulder for a long time, it is easy for your opponent to pull his hand back and escape. Therefore, once you apply this control you should look for another technique to control him more securely.

Escape and Counter: When you sense your right hand has been covered, simply pull it back or pull his shoulder back. This will stop him from

Figure 4-99.

Figure 4-100.

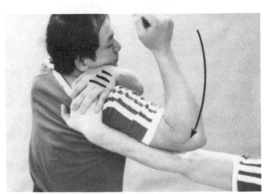

Figure 4-101.

Figure 4-102.

doing his technique. To counter this technique, use your left hand to grab his right forearm (Figure 4-103) and bend it backward while pulling your right hand back to lock his forearm (Figure 4-104). You may also add a finger Chin Na to increase his pain.

8. Ing Shyong Yeou Lii (The Hero Shows Courtesy) 英雄有禮
Technique #36: This technique is similar to Technique #35, the only difference being that your opponent is in front of you instead of in back. When he touches your left shoulder with his right hand, cover his hand with your right hand and raise your left elbow over his forearm (Figure 4-105). Then press your elbow down while bowing forward (Figure 4-106), until his face touches the floor.
Principle: Dividing the muscle/tendon in the wrist and misplacing the bone in the elbow. Unlike Technique #35, this technique can be used for a permanent control because your body is in a better position.
Escape and Counter: When you find your opponent intends to control you with this technique, you can either simply pull your hand back or else

Figure 4-103.

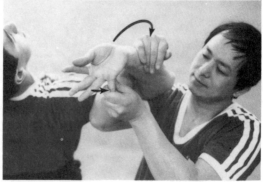

Figure 4-104.

Figure 4-105.

Figure 4-106.

pull his body forward to destroy his balance. This will stop him from controlling you. To counterattack, first push his elbow up with your left hand (Figure 4-107), and while his mind is on his elbow, quickly circle your right hand around his neck. Pull his neck forward and downward while pushing his elbow backward to lock him (Figure 4-108).

9. Yeu Wo Torng Shyng (Walk With Me) 與我同行

Technique #37: This technique is also used by police to control criminals without handcuffs. There are many ways to approach this Chin Na. Whenever you have a chance to grab the opponent's right hand with your left hand (Figure 4-109), immediately take over the control with your right hand (4-110). Then step your left leg behind his right leg, move your left arm under his armpit, and lock his right thumb with your left thumb (Figure 4-111). Finally, push your left thumb out while pressing your left palm to the back of his hand to increase the pain (Figure Figure 4-112). You must apply enough pressure so that his heels leave the floor.

Principle: Dividing the muscle/tendon. Practically speaking, it is very hard to do this technique. The entire process takes too much time, and your opponent can easily sense your intention. This technique is usually only done in a fight when you are using stick and adhere.

Escape and Counter: Once you have sensed the opponent's intention,

Figure 4-107.

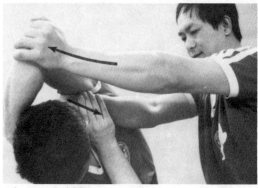

Figure 4-108.

Figure 4-109.

Figure 4-110.

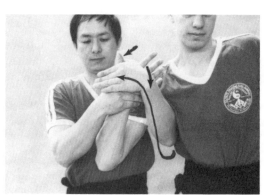

Figure 4-111.

Figure 4-112.

pull your hand back as soon as possible and at the same time pull your elbow in to prevent his left arm from locking your elbow. For a counterattack, since your opponent must use two hands to set up the technique and the range is so close, you can easily use your left hand to punch him and force him to stop the technique and protect himself. Alternatively, you can use your left hand to lock his left thumb (Figures 4-113 and 4-114).

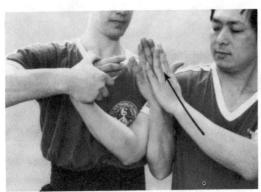

Figure 4-113.

Figure 4-114.

CHAPTER 5

ELBOW CHIN NA

5-1. Introduction

Generally speaking, elbow Chin Na is harder to use by itself than finger or wrist Chin Na, because the elbow is a stronger joint. Let us start with a look at the structure of the elbow joint. In the elbow, the bones are connected by three ligaments: the radial collateral ligament, the ulnar collateral ligament, and the annular ligament (Figure 5-1). Strong tendons and muscles run over the joint (Figure 5-2). Because of the structure, the muscles and tendons are more moveable and flexible at this joint. However, the ligaments are less flexible and are more easily torn from the bone when pressure is applied at the right angle. On the other hand, when the tendons and muscles are tensed up, they can easily protect the ligaments from being damaged. For this reason, the major principle used for elbow control is misplacing the bone. Dividing the muscle/tendon is usually a minor effect in elbow control.

Because the elbow is stronger than the other two joints already discussed, you need more strength to apply the technique. If your opponent stiffens his arm and tightens his muscles, it is very difficult to apply the technique. You must therefore be very skillful and fast. Right before he senses your intention and stiffens his arm, you should already control him. Alternatively, you may also make him lose his balance first and while he is worrying about his balance, take this opportunity and control him. For this reason stepping is very important in elbow and shoulder Chin Na. You must use stepping to generate a large circle to make him lose his balance.

To control the elbow, you have to be at a closer range than is the case with finger and wrist Chin Na. Most of the finger and wrist Chin Na can be done at long or middle range to prevent the opponent from punching or kicking you. This option is not open if you intend to control the opponent's elbow. To prevent your opponent from punching or kicking you, you must step to his side or rear.

You will find that most of the elbow Chin Na require a skillful wrist Chin Na first. If there is no good wrist Chin Na, the elbow Chin Na will be ineffective and dangerous to you. Wrist Chin Na and elbow Chin Na

Figure 5-1.   Figure 5-2.

cooperate and react like brothers, helping each other to make the control safer and more effective. For this reason it is often very difficult to tell what category this kind of Chin Na should belong to. Sometimes the wrist is used for control while the elbow is used for locking, other times the wrist is used for locking while elbow Chin Na is used for controlling. Moreover, occasionally you will see techniques which control the wrist, elbow, and shoulder all at the same time.

5-2. Elbow Chin Na Techniques
A. Charn Joow (Elbow Wrap) 纏肘
1. Shao Charn Joow (Small Elbow Wrap) 小纏肘
Technique #38: When your enemy punches you or grabs you with his right hand (Figure 5-3), use your right hand to grab his wrist while using your left forearm to press his elbow up (Figure 5-4). While you are doing this you should also step your left leg to the front of his right leg. Then bend forward, pulling his hand toward you and pushing his elbow forward and down (Figure 5-5). If you want to make your opponent fall, you can also sweep your left leg backward while your left arm is pressing down (Figure 5-6), and then control his arm on his back (Figure 5-7).
Principle: Misplacing the bone. This technique can also be used to dislocate the shoulder joint when the pressure is applied at the right angle (Figure 5-8).
Escape and Counter: To prevent your elbow from being locked, you must pull your arm back to your chest immediately and also turn your body to face him. This puts him in an awkward position to control you and also makes him worry about your left punch. To counter, you can push his left elbow up with your left hand while grabbing his right wrist with your right hand (Figure 5-9). Then move your body to his rear and lock both his arms above his left shoulder (Figure 5-10).

2. Da Charn Joow (Large Elbow Wrap) 大纏肘
Technique #39: This technique is used for offense. First grab your opponent's left wrist with your right hand, pressing your palm forward to force his elbow up (Figure 5-11). This will set him up and prevent him

Figure 5-3.

Figure 5-4.

Figure 5-5.

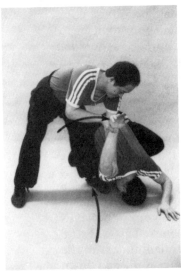

Figure 5-6.

Figure 5-7.

Figure 5-8.

Figure 5-9.

Figure 5-10.

Figure 5-11.   Figure 5-12.   Figure 5-13.

from stiffening his arm. Then step your left leg to his left as you use your
left forearm to lock his elbow (Figure 5-12). Finally, step your right leg to
his rear, turn your body to your left, and the same time press his shoulder
down (Figure 5-13). If you need to injure him to stop the fight, you can
push your right hand forward and dislocate his shoulder (Figure 5-14).
When you control your opponent you must force his face to the floor in
order to prevent him from rolling over and escaping.

Principle: Misplacing the bone at the elbow and shoulder, and dividing
the muscle at the wrist. This technique is a combination of wrist, elbow,
and shoulder Chin Na. However, because the key to success is the
wrapping of the elbow it is included in the elbow category. Stepping is
important in this technique. You must use stepping to the opponent's side
and then rear to keep him from punching or kicking you.

Escape and Counter: The first reaction when you sense your opponent's
intention is to stiffen your wrist and pull your elbow back. This will stop
the technique. If unfortunately you have been controlled almost to the
end, you must roll over onto your back before your face is pushed down
to the floor (Figure 5-15). This will release you from the technique, but
you must immediately pull your arm back before your opponent changes
his strategy and catches you with another technique. To counter, if you
act just when your opponent catches your wrist, you can grab his pinky
with your right hand (Figure 5-16) and bend it down to control him
(Figure 5-17).

3. Faan Charn Joow (Reverse Elbow Wrap) 反纏肘

Technique #40: This technique is very similar to Technique #39, however
the approach and control are somewhat different. First step your left leg
to your opponent's left side while your left hand grabs his left wrist and
raises it up (Figure 5-18). Then step your right leg to his rear as your right
hand passes under his elbow and wraps around his upper arm (Figure 5-
19). Finally, step your left leg to your left and at the same time pull him
down by applying pressure with your right arm (Figure 5-20). Notice that
once you have used your right hand to lock his elbow, you immediately
release his wrist and move your hand to the new position and press his
arm in place. You must control him until his face touches the floor.

Principle: Misplacing the bone both in the elbow and shoulder. In this

Figure 5-14.

Figure 5-15.

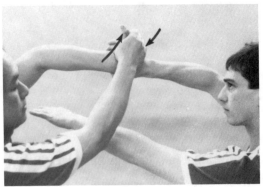

Figure 5-16.

Figure 5-17.

Figure 5-18.

Figure 5-19.

Figure 5-20.

Figure 5-21.

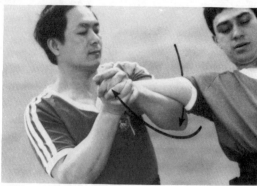

Figure 5-22.

Figure 5-23.

Figure 5-24.

technique you must move him in a circle to make him lose his balance. This will prevent him from attacking you with his other hand.

Escape and Counter: When your left wrist is grabbed, push his left hand away with your right hand while turning your body to your left. This will stop him from controlling you. To counter, before he presses you down, immediately grab your left wrist with your right hand (Figure 5-21) and scoop your left arm up to lock his elbow (Figure 5-22).

4. Shang Charn Joow (Upward Elbow Wrap) 上纏肘

Technique #41: This technique can be used as a counterattack against a punch. If your opponent punches with his right hand, intercept it with a left hand covering technique (Figure 5-23), and then grab his wrist with both of your hands (Figure 5-24). Twist his hand to your left with your left hand and circle it counterclockwise as your right hand slides under his tricep. Press your left hand down and at the same time lift your right hand up until his heels leave the floor (Figures 5-25 and 5-26). As you are doing this you should also slide your legs to his side to prevent him from punching with his left hand.

Principle: Dividing the muscle/tendon in the wrist and misplacing the bone in the elbow. In this technique the wrist acts as the major control while the elbow only locks and sets the arm up.

Escape and Counter: Once you sense your opponent's intention; immediately pull your elbow back to your chest so that he cannot lock your elbow with his right hand. Watch out for a possible punch when you are pulling your arm back. To counter, pull your right elbow back, grab his left hand with your left hand (Figure 5-27), and twist your body to your left, using your elbow to press his left elbow down (Figure 5-28).

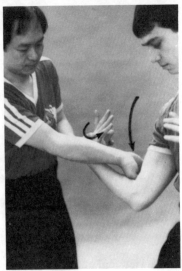

Figure 5-25.

Figure 5-26.

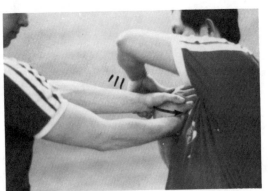

Figure 5-27.

Figure 5-28.

5. Joan Shen Charn Joow (Turning Body Elbow Wrap) 轉身纏肘

Technique #42: This technique if used against an opponent who touches your shoulder or hooks your neck. When you opponent uses his right hand to hook your neck, cover his hand with your right hand and at the same time lift your left arm over his right arm (Figure 5-29). Then rotate your body counterclockwise and step your right leg behind him while your left hand pulls his right elbow to his rear and then up. Your right hand releases his right hand while turning, but grabs it again at the completion of the turn (Figure 5-30). Finally, press your left arm down to control him (Figure 5-31).

Principle: Dividing the muscle/tendon in the wrist and misplacing the bone in the elbow and shoulder. When you do this technique, you must be fast, otherwise your opponent can easy sense your turning and do something against you.

Escape and Counter: Once you sense your opponent's intention, immediately pull your elbow back to your chest. To neutralize his attempt, simply step your left leg forward and face him while pulling your

Figure 5-29.

Figure 5-30.

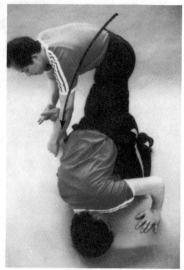
Figure 5-31.

Figure 5-32.

Figure 5-33.

elbow back. To counter, you can simply pull him backward while he is turning.

B. Ya Joow (Elbow Press) 壓肘
1. Shang Ya Joow (Upward Elbow Press) 上壓肘
Technique #43: When your opponent punches with his left hand, intercept it with your right forearm (Figure 5-32). Then coil your right hand around his forearm up to his elbow and grab his wrist with your left hand while moving your body to his left (Figure 5-33). Finally, push his elbow up with your right hand while your left hand holds his hand down (Figure 5-34). You must make him lift his heels off the floor so that he cannot kick you.
Principle: Misplacing the bone. You must use stick and adhere, wrap and coil up. Your arm moves like a snake creeping up a branch. Step to his left and lift his heels off the floor to stop any further attack.
Escape and Counter: Pull your hand back once your punch has been intercepted. When your opponent steps to your left side, step with him so that your are still facing him. Correct stepping will keep him from being able to control you safely. To counterattack, when his right hand is coiling up your arm, grab his right hand with your other hand (Figure 5-35) and apply a wrist Chin Na to control him (Figure 5-36).

Figure 5-35.

Figure 5-34.

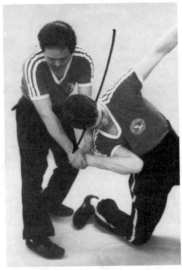

Figure 5-37.

Figure 5-36.

2. Jen Tiao Bian Dan (Carry a Pole on the Shoulder) 肩挑扁担

Technique #44: When your opponent punches with his right hand, intercept and grab his right wrist with your right hand (Figure 5-37). Step your left leg behind his right leg as you extend his arm and place it on either shoulder, his palm facing out so that you can lock it (Figure 5-38 shows left shoulder). Control his other arm with your left arm, and pull his right hand back to lock him (Figures 5-39 and 5-40). You must force his heels off the floor and you must control his left hand with your left hand to prevent him from punching your face.

Principle: Misplacing the bone. Further pressure will misplace the joint. If you cannot prevent his left hand from punching you, then put more pressure on his right hand and dislocate his shoulder.

Escape and Counter: Pull your arm back as soon as possible to keep him from putting it on his shoulder. As you are doing this, twist your arm to an angle where you can bend it. This will stop him from going further. Alternatively, you may use your left hand to push his left elbow forward and pull your right hand backward (Figure 5-41). This will stop him from

Figure 5-38.

Figure 5-39.

Figure 5-40.

Figure 5-41.

Figure 5-42.

continuing the technique. To counter, grab his left wrist with your left hand, which will keep his left arm from reaching your chest, and at the same time place your right forearm on his left elbow (Figure 5-42). Immediately bow forward to control his elbow (Figure 5-43).

3. Shang Jiah Joow (Prop Up Elbow) 上架肘

Technique #45: This is an attack Chin Na. First grab your opponent's right wrist with your right hand (Figure 5-44). Then step your left leg to the opponent's right side as you rotate his arm so that the palm faces up, raising his elbow with your left arm, and finally lift his elbow while pressing his hand down and back (Figure 5-45). Remember that his heels must leave the floor. Stay on his right side and beware of his left hand punch.

Principle: Misplacing the bone. You must set up the right angle for the control, then lifting his elbow and pushing down with your right hand will put him in extreme pain. Step to his right to avoid his left hand punch. If he can punch you with his left hand, your position must be wrong.

Figure 5-43.

Figure 5-44.

Figure 5-45.

Figure 5-46.

Escape and Counter: Pull in your elbow immediately to keep his left elbow from controlling you, and at the same time use your left hand to punch his face before he steps to your right and completely controls you. There are many techniques for counterattack, one of which is using your left hand to grab and push his left hand toward him while your are pulling his right hand to your right (Figure 5-46). Then rotate his arms and lock them in place (Figure 5-47).

4. Sou Wou Da Liang (Hands Holding a Large Beam) 手握大樑
Technique #46: Grab your opponent's right wrist with your right hand and pull it to your right (Figure 5-48). Then step to his right and move your left hand over his arm and hook it under his elbow (Figure 5-49). Lift his elbow up as you push his hand down.
Principle: Misplacing the bone. If you are taller than your opponent you will find this technique easy to use. However, if you are shorter, this technique will not be practical since your opponent can easily punch your face with his left hand.

Figure 5-47.

Figure 5-48.

Figure 5-49.

Figure 5-50.

Escape and Counter: Your first reaction should be to pull your hand back and bend your elbow before he locks it, while at the same time punching his face with your left hand. To counter, you can use any wrist Chin Na technique on him. Alternatively, you can use your left hand to push his left elbow forward while you grab his right wrist and pull it backward (Figure 5-50), and then lock his pinky with your right hand and raise him up (Figure 5-51).

5. Shiah Ya Joow (Low Elbow Press) 下壓肘
Technique #47: This technique can be used against any wrist grab. If your opponent grasps your right wrist with his right hand, cover his hand with your left hand as if you were doing the small wrap hand technique (Technique #18)(Figure 5-52), then pull his arm straight while placing your left elbow over his elbow (Figure 5-53). Finally, raise your hands while lowering your elbow as you sit down in your stance (Figure 5-54). You must hold his hand in the correct angle so that you will be able to keep his elbow straight and lock his arm, otherwise he will be able to

Figure 5-51.

Figure 5-52.

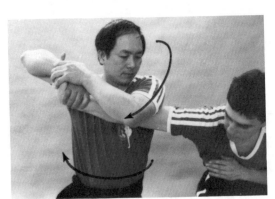
Figure 5-53.

Figure 5-54.

escape. Remember to bring him down so that his left elbow touches the floor.

Principle: Misplacing the bone. It is important to do the wrist Chin Na correctly and in coordination with the elbow technique. As a matter of fact, when you are comfortable with this technique the dividing the muscle/tendon in the wrist will be as important as the elbow technique. If you wish to inflict more pain, you can add a finger Chin Na.

Escape and Counter: The first reaction is to keep your arm bent by withdrawing your elbow. This will pull him into range of your left punch. You can then punch his face or use a wrist Chin Na to counter. Remember your opponent has an equal chance to punch you while you are withdrawing your elbow. To counter, you may use your left hand to lock his right pinky (Figure 5-55) and press the pinky to the side while pressing his wrist down with your right hand (Figure 5-56).

6. Lao Hoann Bay Jiang (Old Man Promoted to General) 老漢拜將
Technique #48: This technique is similar to Technique #46 and is also commonly used to counterattack against a wrist grab. When your opponent uses his left hand to grasp your right wrist, cover his hand with your left hand as in Technique #19, and raise your hands in front of your face (Figure 5-57). Notice that his wrist rests in the "Tiger's Mouth"

Figure 5-55.

Figure 5-56.

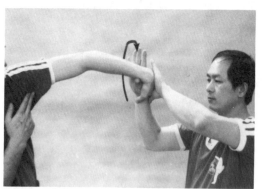

Figure 5-57.

Figure 5-58.

between the thumb and index finger of your right hand. Rotate your body as you place your right elbow over his elbow (Figure 5-58), and then press down (Figure 5-59). As in the previous technique, his arm must be in the right angle so that you can keep his arm straight and lock it, and you must press him to the floor.

Principle: Misplacing the bone. Refer to Technique #46.

Escape and Counter: As soon as you sense the opponent's intention, bend your elbow and use your other hand to push his elbow away. This will stop him from controlling you. To counter, grab his left hand with your right hand, and at the same time bend your left elbow to prevent him from covering it with his elbow (Figure 5-60). Then step your right leg to his left while circling your left hand to lock and control his left elbow (Figure 5-61).

7. Tzuoo Yow Jiau Joow (Left Right Cross Elbow) 左右交肘
Technique #49: This technique is used whenever you find your opponent's arms crossed, or when you cause him to cross his arms. Grasp his right wrist with your right hand, as in this instance when you intercept a chest punch (Figure 5-62), and pull his hand down to expose your face area (Figure 5-63), which will cause him to punch your face with his left hand (Figure 5-64). When this happens, grab his hand with your left hand and immediately cross his arms so that you can control him (Figure 5-65).

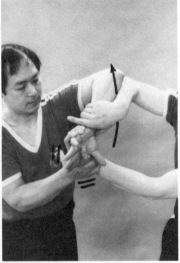

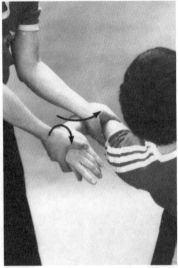

Figure 5-59.　　　　　Figure 5-60.　　　　　Figure 5-61.

Figure 5-62.　　　　　　　　Figure 5- 63.

Figure 5-64.

Figure 5-65.

Figure 5-66.

Figure 5-67.

Figure 5-68.

Figure 5-69.

Figure 5-70.

Principle: Misplacing the bone. In this technique you use the opponent's arm to press his own elbow. Press him until his is off balance, and beware of a possible kick.

Escape and Counter: Once your wrist has been grasped, use wrist Chin Na to control him or use the escape techniques which are used against a wrist control as discussed earlier. Another option for counterattack once both your wrists are grabbed is to pull his left arm to his right and use the same technique to control him. You will have as good a chance of success as your opponent.

天旋地轉 - 1

8. Tien Hsuen Di Joan-1 (The Heavens Turn and the Earth Circles-1)
Technique #50: When someone grabs your shirt from behind (Figure 5-66), simply turn right to face him and raise both arms . Use your right arm to press his arm to your neck while locking his elbow with your left arm (Figure 5-67). Then bow forward while pressing your arm down on his elbow (Figure 5-68).

Principle: Misplacing the bone. When you apply this technique you must be fast, otherwise your opponent can easily sense your intention and pull you backward off balance.

Escape and Counter: Pull your arm straight back before he can lock you. You may also pull him down while he is turning. To counter, you can use your left hand to grab his left wrist (Figure 5-69) and use a wrist Chin Na on him (Figures 5-70 and 5-71).

Figure 5-71.

Figure 5-72.

Figure 5-73.

Figure 5-74.

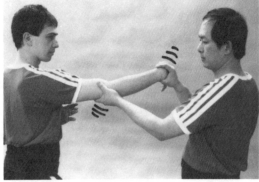

Figure 5-75.

天旋地轉 — 2

9. Tien Hsuen Di Joan-2 (The Heavens Turn and the Earth Circles-2)
Technique #51: When someone grabs your shirt from behind, turn to your left and lock his right elbow with your left arm (Figure 5-72). Then bow forward and at the same time press his elbow down (Figure 5-73).
Principle: Misplacing the bone. Refer to Technique #50.
Escape and Counter: Pull your arm straight back before he can lock you. You may also pull him down while he is turning. To counter, you can use your left hand to grab his left wrist while he is turning and use a wrist Chin Na on him (Figure 5-74).

C. Joan Joow (Turning Elbow) 轉肘
1. Chyan Fan Joow (Forward Turning Elbow) 前翻肘
Technique #52: This technique is commonly used as a takedown. Whenever you have a chance to grab your opponent's right wrist with your right hand, grab his elbow with your other hand (Figure 5-75), then rotate his hand to his right rear as you pull his elbow toward you (Figure 5-76). While you are rotating his arm, step your right leg behind his right

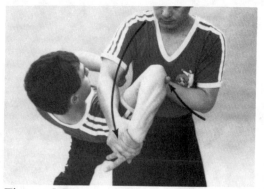

Figure 5-76.

Figure 5-77.

Figure 5-78.

Figure 5-79.

leg. If necessary, you may slide your right leg backward to make him fall easily.

Principle: Misplacing the bone. It is hard to maintain control with this technique for any length of time, so usually you will just make the opponent fall so that you can use some other technique, or else pop his elbow out of joint.

Escape and Counter: Use one of the wrist escape techniques to get out of the grab. To counter, you may first sink your right elbow while using your left hand to push his right elbow up (Figure 5-77), then grab his right wrist and press him down to the floor (Figure 5-78).

2. Shy Tzu Yao Tao (Lion Shakes its Head) 獅子搖頭

Technique #53: This technique is commonly used against a grab on your arm or elbow such as is commonly applied in Judo. When your opponent's left hand grabs your right elbow or arm (Figure 5-79), simply cover his left hand with your left hand (Figure 5-80). Then circle your right hand around his arm and twist your body to your left while your left hand controls his wrist and your right hand controls his elbow (Figure 5-81).

Principle: Misplacing the bone. When you use this technique, remember that he can punch or kick you from his right side.

Figure 5-80.

Figure 5-81.

Figure 5-82.

Figure 5-83.

Escape and Counter: Since your opponent has to use both hands to apply the technique, you can easily punch his face or even kick him if you act before you are completely controlled. To counter, you may use your right hand to grab his left wrist (Figure 5-82), then turn your body to your right and control his left wrist with both hands (Figure 5-83). Finally, twist and bend his hand to increase the pain on his wrist and raise him up (Figure 5-84).

3. Chyan Shang Fan (Forward Upward Turning) 前上翻

Technique #54: This technique can be used against a chest grab or a right hand punch. When your opponent punches your chest with his right hand, intercept with your left hand and lock his elbow with your right hand (Figure 5-85). Then pull your elbow toward you while pushing his wrist forward to lock his arm. You can clasp your hands to make your control firmer (Figure 5-86).

Principle: Misplacing the bone. Remember to step your right leg to your opponent's right to prevent him from punching you with his left hand, or step behind his right leg in case you want to sweep his leg and make him fall backwards.

Escape and Counter: Use your left hand to push his right arm away and at the same time pull your right hand back. This will stop his attempt to control you. To counter, you may pull your right elbow in to your chest

Figure 5-84.

Figure 5-85.

Figure 5-86.

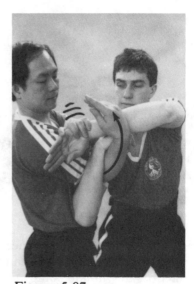

Figure 5-87.

and at the same time use your left hand to grab his left hand (Figure 5-87). Then use your left hand to twist his left wrist while straightening your right arm to lock him (Figure 5-88).

4. How Sharn Fan (Backward Upward Turning) 後上翻

Technique #55: This technique is used against a wrist control. When your right wrist is grabbed by the opponent's right hand (Figure 5-89), hold his hand with your left hand and move your elbow over his elbow to set his arm up for control (Figure 5-90). Continue circling your elbow around his elbow and lift it to your rear until he loses his balance (Figure 5-91).

Principle: Dividing the muscle/tendon for the wrist and misplacing the bone for the elbow. Remember to step your right leg to his right side to prevent him from punching you with his left hand.

Escape and Counter: You can use the following technique either for escape or counter. Before your opponent's elbow locks your elbow, simply push his elbow up with your left hand (Figure 5-92). Then use your right hand to press up his right wrist and lock him up (Figure 5-93).

Figure 5-88.

Figure 5-89.

Figure 5-90.

Figure 5-91.

Figure 5-92.

Figure 5-93.

Figure 5-94.

Figure 5-95.

Figure 5-96.

Figure 5-97.

Figure 5-98.

5. Lao Hoann Bai Yu (Old Man Carries Fish on his Back) 老漢背魚
Technique #56: Whenever you have a chance to grab your opponent's right wrist with your right hand, or when he grabs your right wrist with his right hand (Figure 5-94), grab his right wrist with your left hand, turn your body to the right, and place his elbow on your shoulder (Figure 5-95). Finally, bend forward to lock him in place (Figure 5-96). Pull down with both hands until his heels leave the floor.

Principle: Dividing the muscle/tendon and misplacing the bone for both elbow and shoulder. This technique is a large circle and it is easily sensed by the opponent. It is not easy to use this technique in a real fight.

Escape and Counter: Simply stiffen your arm and pull it back. To counter, while your opponent is turning his body, you also turn with him and at the same time use your left hand to grab his left hand (Figure 5-97), and then twist his left wrist and pull him backward to make him fall (Figure 5-98). Alternatively, while he is turning, grab his left wrist with your left hand and at the same time grab his pinky with your right (Figure 5-99). Bend his pinky down to control him (Figure 5-100).

Figure 5-99.

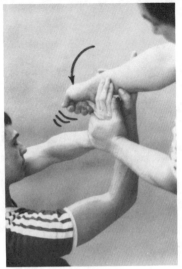

Figure 5-100.

Figure 5-101.

Figure 5-102.

6. Hui Tao Chin Yuan (Turn Back to Seize the Ape) 回頭擒猿

Technique #57: This technique is used to control an opponent who is using his left hand to grab your right shoulder from behind. Whenever your shoulder is touched, your first reaction should be to cover his hand with your other hand (Figure 5-101) and turn your body while circling your right arm over his elbow (Figure 5-102). Finally, extend your right arm and push his chest with your hand (Figure 5-103). This will increase the pain and stop him from turning.

Principle: Misplacing the bone in the elbow and dividing the muscle/tendon in the shoulder. This technique is fast and effective. Unfortunately, in a real fight no one will touch your shoulder from the rear since he can punch you just as easily.

Escape and Counter: In this technique it is pretty hard for your opponent to effectively cover your hand so you cannot escape. You can easily pull your hand back before your elbow is locked. To counter you can use your left hand to grab his left wrist (Figure 5-104), then twist his wrist down while stiffening your left arm to control his shoulder (Figure 5-105).

7. Lao Hoann Yeou Lii (Old Man Bows Politely) 老漢有禮

Technique #58: This technique is used against a grab to your waist area from the rear. When your opponent uses his right hand to grab your waist from the rear, grab his hand with your right hand (Figure 5-106), turn

Figure 5-103.

Figure 5-104.

Figure 5-105.

Figure 5-106.

Figure 5-107.

your body to your left and lock his elbow with your left arm (Figure 5-107) and then push your left elbow down to control him (Figure 5-108).
Principle: Misplacing the bone in the shoulder. This technique is not practical, because in a real fight no one will grab your back when he can just as easily punch you.

Escape and Counter: When he first tries to grab your hand you can easily pull it back. Alternatively, you can use your right hand to pull him backward and make him lose his balance. This will stop him from doing any technique.

8. Shuang Sou Chin Shiong (Both Hands Seize the Murderer) 双手擒凶
Technique #59: When your enemy punches you with his right hand, first intercept his punch with your right hand, grab the wrist and press it down (Figure 5-109). Then coil your left hand to his elbow (Figure 5-110). You can then release your right hand and press his shoulder upward to increase the pain (Figure 5-111). Alternatively, you may use your right arm to choke him and make him pass out (Figure 5-112). Remember

Figure 5-108.

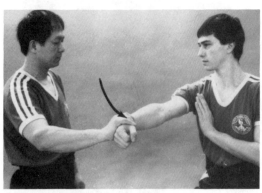

Figure 5-109.

Figure 5-110.

Figure 5-111.

when your left arm is coiling to his elbow to also step behind him.

Principle: Misplacing the bone in the elbow and dividing the muscle/tendon in the shoulder.

Escape and Counter: It is hard for your opponent to set you up in the proper position, so before you are completely controlled you can easily step away and pull your arm out of his lock. Alternatively, while he steps behind your back, you can step with him, moving your right arm out of his control. To counter, while his left hand coils to your elbow, simply hook your right arm up with the help of your left hand to lock his elbow (Figure 5-113).

Figure 5-112.

Figure 5-113.

第 六 章
肩、頸、腰擒拿

CHAPTER 6
SHOULDER, NECK, AND
WAIST CHIN NA

6-1. Introduction

In the last few chapters you have seen that there are advantages and disadvantages to the various Chin Na used on the different parts of the body. To use a technique effectively you must be fast and skillful, and must step to the right place at the right time. From the simple and effective finger Chin Na (small circle), to the elbow Chin Na (medium circle), and now to shoulder Chin Na (large circle), every technique has it's own characteristics and it's particular application. One technique may be good for attack, another may be more effective as a counterattack or a follow-up attack.

It is hard to say which technique is best, or which portion of the opponent's body it is better to control in a fight, for everything depends on the situation and your reaction to it. When the time, distance, and situation are right, any technique can be the right one. **WHEN THE SITUATION HAPPENS, YOU DO NOT HAVE TIME TO THINK. YOU MUST REACT NATURALLY.** In order to reach this level, you must ceaselessly practice, discuss, and ponder.

In this chapter, in addition to shoulder Chin Na we will also introduce body Chin Na, which includes the neck, and waist Chin Na. You will find that these techniques are not as easy to use as the Chin Na shown in the last few chapters. The main reason for this is that they are not applied to the hands and arms, but rather to the body itself. Theoretically speaking, if your hands are able to reach the opponent's shoulder and body, you can just as easily punch him as control him. But by the same token, if your hands are able to reach the opponent's body, his arms can reach you just as easily. In addition, to control the shoulder or body you need more muscle and speed simply because the shoulder is stronger than the arm, and the waist is stronger than the other joints. For these reasons, there is only a limited number of techniques used on the body. In this chapter, shoulder Chin Na will be introduced first, followed by neck and waist

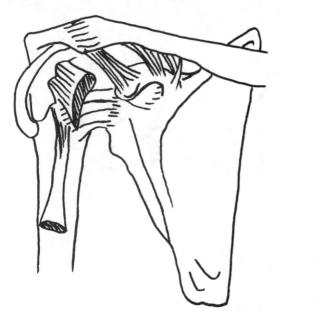

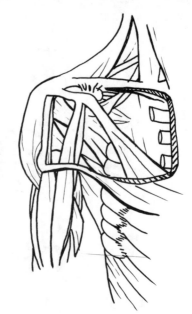

Figure 6-1.   Figure 6-2.

Chin Na. Usually, the neck and waist Chin Na are not classified in any of the circle Chin Na simply because circular motion is not absolutely required for them.

6-2. Shoulder Chin Na Techniques

Before we discuss shoulder Chin Na, let us look at the structure of the shoulder. The shoulder joint is connected by two major ligaments: the capsular ligament and the coracoacromial ligament (Figure 6-1), and there are various tendons and muscles on top of the ligaments (Figure 6-2). Because of the similarity to the elbow, shoulder Chin Na follows the same principles as elbow Chin Na. Most of the techniques are for misplacing the bone.

Generally speaking, it is harder to use Chin Na on the shoulder than on the fingers, wrist, or elbow. There are several reasons for this. First, the shoulder joint is much stronger than the finger, wrist, or elbow, so more power is required to make a technique work. Second, to control the shoulder you have to be closer to the opponent, which means that he has a better chance to punch or kick you as you are trying to apply the technique. Shoulder techniques are therefore more dangerous to apply. Third, in order to apply shoulder Chin Na safely, you must either use stepping to keep away from your opponent's punches, or you have to make him lose his balance first. This extra movement means that shoulder techniques are large circle Chin Na, and as such they require more time than the medium or small circle techniques. This extra time unfortunately gives your opponent a chance to se nse your intention and defend against you.

Because of these reasons, shoulder Chin Na is not commonly used in the styles which emphasize mainly punching and kicking or long range fighting. However, shoulder Chin Na is used in the styles which emphasize short range fighting and sticking and adhering, such as Chinese wrestling, White Crane, Snake, or internal styles such as Tai Chi Chuan.

Figure 6-3.

Figure 6-4.

In this section we will introduce only a few of the common shoulder Chin Na which are relatively practical in use. However, you should understand that, as mentioned in the last chapter, many elbow Chin Na also control the shoulder at the same time. By the same token, many shoulder Chin Na also control the elbow.

Shoulder Chin Na:
A. Shang Diing (Upward Press) 上頂
1. Yi Juh Diing Tien (One Post to Support the Heavens) 一柱頂天
Technique #60: Whenever you have a chance to grab your opponent's right wrist with your right hand (Figure 6-3), pull his arm straight and at the same time step your left leg in front of him and place your shoulder under his armpit (Figure 6-4). His palm must face up to lock the elbow. Pull down with both your hands and then lift his arm up (Figure 6-5). This lifting will cause him great pain.
Principle: Misplacing the bone in the shoulder. Straightening his arm, pulling it downward, and then lifting it up sets up the correct angle for dislocating his shoulder.
Escape and Counter: When you sense your opponent's intention, immediately pull your elbow in and push his shoulder away with your left hand and rotate your body to his front. This will free you from his control. To counter, first push his shoulder forward with your left hand while pulling your elbow in (Figure 6-6). Then grab his left hand with your left hand (Figure 6-7). Finally, as you twist his left wrist, push his neck to your right with your right hand to increase the pain (Figure 6-8).

2. Bei Ping Kao Ya (Roast Peking Duck) 北平烤鴨
Technique #61: This technique controls both the elbow and the shoulder. Whenever you have a chance to hold the opponent's wrist or hand (Figure 6-9), twist your hand counterclockwise to turn his palm to the right and keep his elbow bent, and simultaneously move your left hand under his right arm to hook his neck (Figure 6-10). While doing this, you should also step your left leg to his right. Finally, rotate his arm until his palm faces up, then press your right hand down while lifting your left elbow up by pressing down on his neck, and force him up on his toes (Figure 6-11).
Principle: Misplacing the bone. If you use more force than needed to

Figure 6-5.

Figure 6-6.

Figure 6-7.

Figure 6-8.

Figure 6-9.

Figure 6-10.

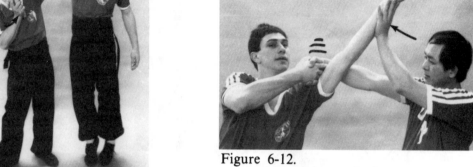

Figure 6-12.

Figure 6-11.

control him, you can either break his elbow or dislocate his shoulder. You must control him until his heels leave the floor, otherwise he can still kick or punch you.

Escape and Counter: Your opponent's key to controlling you is to lock your elbow. Therefore, in order to escape you must first prevent your elbow from being locked. When your opponent turns your right palm up, immediately pull your hand in and bend your elbow. This will stop his control. Naturally, while your are pulling your right hand back you can also kick him or use your left hand to punch him. To counter, you may use your left hand to stop his left hand while it is attempting to hold your neck (Figure 6-12), and then pull his right arm to your right while pushing his left hand toward him, and immediately lock his arms in position (Figure 6-13).

B. Shiah Ya (Low Press) 下壓
1. Shuang Torng Bai For (Two Children Worship the Buddha) 雙童拜佛
Technique #62: When you have a chance to grab your opponent's right wrist with your right hand (Figure 6-14), pull his hand to your right, and at the same time step your left leg to his right while your left hand moves under his right arm and across his body to control his left arm (Figure 6-15). Then pull your right hand toward your body and at the same time press your left shoulder downward while bowing forward (Figure 6-16).
Principle: Misplacing the bone. This technique can temporarily control your opponent. It would be very hard to dislocate the shoulder or elbow since you do not have enough space to move and increase your controlling pressure.
Escape and Counter: In order for your opponent to control you, he must stand side by side with you. Therefore, you can simply pull your right arm back while stepping your left leg to his front in order to prevent him from controlling you. To counter, you should first sink your elbow and at the same time cover his right hand with your left hand (Figure 6-17), and then use the small wrap hand technique to press him down (Figure 6-18).

2. Ing Shyong Kuah Hwu (Hero Rides the Tiger) 英雄跨虎
Technique #63: This is a shoulder control used when your opponent is on the ground. When you can grasp the opportunity, sit on his shoulder

Figure 6-13.

Figure 6-14.

Figure 6-15.

Figure 6-16.

while locking his neck with your leg, and pull his arm back (Figure 6-19). This will cause extreme pain in his shoulder. You may also add a finger Chin Na to increase the pain. Refer to Chapter 7 for techniques to make your opponent fall.

Principle: Misplacing the bone. This technique is very useful in controlling an opponent once he is on the ground. You can lock him so he can't move and you can also dislocate or break the shoulder joint. However, if you do not set him up right he can still bite you.

Escape and Counter: When you are on the ground you should get up as soon as possible. If you can't get up at once, you should face up so that you can see your opponent, and try to kick or punch him to keep him from reaching your body.

C. Tseh Diing (Side Press) 側頂
1. Yeang Tien Charng Shiaw (Look to the Heavens and Shout) 仰天長嘯
Technique #64: This technique is similar to Technique #62 except that you move your left arm over his right arm to reach his neck, instead of under, and then pull your right hand back against your chest while your left hand presses his neck (Figure 6-20).
Principle: Misplacing the bone for the shoulder and elbow, and sealing the breath for the neck. Stepping to the side is the key to this control.

Figure 6-17.

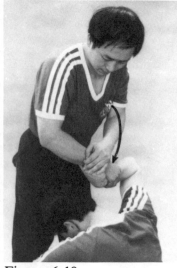
Figure 6-18.

Figure 6-19.

Figure 6-20.

Figure 6-21.

Escape and Counter: Refer to Technique #62. To counter, you may use your left hand to stop his left hand from reaching your neck (Figure 6-21), pull his right hand to your right while pushing his left arm toward him (Figure 6-22), and finally, twist his left wrist and bow forward to control him (Figure 6-23).

6-3. Neck Chin Na Techniques

First let us take a look of the structure of the neck. In the back of the neck is the spine, made up of seven pieces of bone connected with interspinous ligament and posterior atlantoaxial ligament (Figure 6-24). On top of the ligaments are muscles (Figure 6-25). When the neck is twisted to the side and bent backward, these joints can be broken to cause death. On the two sides of the neck are the carotid arteries, which carry oxygen and other supplies to the brain (Figure 6-26). When the supply of blood is stopped for 5 seconds or more, a person can lose consciousness. If the brain is deprived of oxygen for more than a few minutes, it will be

Figure 6-22.

Figure 6-23.

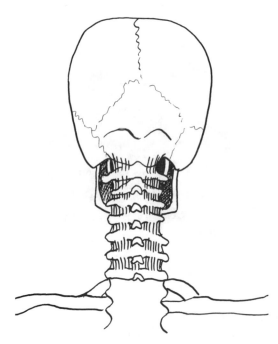

Figure 6-24.

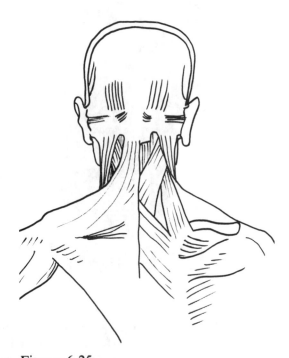

Figure 6-25.

damaged, and death may result. The muscles in the back of the neck are strong, but when they are struck the contraction of the muscles can shock the brain and cause unconsciousness. The neck is also the pathway through which air passes from the nose to the lungs. If the front of the neck is sealed, oxygen will not get to the lungs and death may result. Because of all these reasons, the neck has been considered one of the major targets in a fight. However, due to the structure of the neck, most of the techniques developed are either sealing the vein or sealing the breath. Only a few techniques have been developed to control or lock the neck.

As mentioned in the beginning of this chapter, since many of the neck Chin Na do not require circular motion, especially sealing the breath and

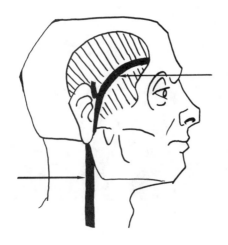

Figure 6-27.

Figure 6-26.

sealing the vein/artery, neck Chin Na cannot be classified as one of the circle Chin Na. However, most Chin Na which control the neck still need some circular motion to do the job.

Generally, neck Chin Na can be classified into four categories: breaking the neck, locking the neck, sealing the breath, and sealing the vein/artery. Breaking the neck Chin Na cannot be easily used to control the opponent, because usually you must either break his neck or withdraw immediately to prevent him from counterattacking you. Locking the neck Chin Na are, of course, used to lock your opponent's neck, although in some cases you can also use the technique to break the neck if necessary. Sealing the breath Chin Na stops the opponent from inhaling, so naturally the windpipe is the target. There are other sealing the breath techniques which do not use the neck, but these will be discussed in a later chapter. As was mentioned in the first chapter, when you apply a sealing the vein/artery technique to the neck it can stop the oxygen supply to the brain and thus cause the opponent to pass out or even die. There are certain sealing the vein/artery techniques which utilize points on your opponent's body to cause an organ or the brain to malfunction. These are not to be confused with sealing the meridian, which causes the opponent's Chi to circulate abnormally. Both of these are classified as cavity press techniques, which will be briefly introduced in a later chapter.

Neck Chin Na:
A. Duan Jiing (Breaking the Neck) 斷勁
1. Sha Ji Neou Tao (Twist the Head to Kill a Chicken) 殺雞扭頭
Technique #65: When your opponent punches you with his right hand, intercept with your right hand and grab his wrist. Pull his arm down while locking his elbow with your left hand (Figure 6-27). Step your right leg behind his right leg, use your left hand to grab his hair or hold his neck, and at the same time place your right hand on his chin. Finally, twist his neck with both hands to the side and back to break the neck (Figure 6-28). Usually a jerking impulse is necessary to break the neck. When you do

Figure 6-28.

Figure 6-29.

Figure 6-30.

Figure 6-31.

Figure 6-32.

this, remember to keep your body close to his right arm, otherwise he might be able to strike you with his elbow.

Principle: Misplacing the bone. When the neck is twisted to the side and backward, the neck can be broken easily.

Escape and Counter: Since your opponent has to use both hands to do the breaking, use your left hand to stop his right hand from reaching your chin, and at the same time step your left leg forward and turn your body to the right (Figure 6-29). This will stop him from further action. To counterattack, use both hands to lock his right arm and bend him backward (Figure 6-30).

B. Suoo Jiing (Locking the Neck) 鎖頭
1. Chyang Poh Jyu Gong (Force the Bow) 強迫翔躬
Technique #66: Whenever you have a chance to grab or intercept and grab your opponent's right wrist, pull his arm to your right and at the same time step your left leg behind him (Figure 6-31). Slide your left arm under his left armpit and lock his neck (Figure 6-32), then immediately

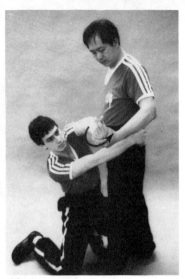

Figure 6-33.   Figure 6-34.   Figure 6-35.

move your right hand under his right armpit to his neck, and press his neck down with both hands (Figure 6-33). Remember, when you lock his neck you should place one leg forward to prevent him from kicking you.

Principle: Dividing the muscle/tendon. This technique can be used to lock the opponent's shoulder and neck, but it is not effective for breaking the neck. When enough pressure is applied, the muscles in the back of the neck will be injured and the windpipe sealed, causing the opponent to pass out.

Escape and Counter: Whenever your right wrist is grabbed, step your left leg forward and turn your body to face your opponent. This will prevent him from controlling either your shoulder or neck from your right side. To counter, you may use your left hand to grab his left hand behind your neck (Figure 6-34), and then twist your body to your left while controlling his wrist (Figure 6-35). Finally, press his elbow down with your right hand until his face touches the ground (Figure 6-36).

2. Neou Sou Ya Jiing (Twist the Arm and Press the Neck): 扭手壓頸
Technique #67: When you have a chance to grab the opponent's right hand or wrist with your right hand (Figure 6-37), lock his neck with your left hand from underneath his arm (Figure 6-38). Then twist your right hand counterclockwise while your left hand presses his neck down (Figure 6-39). Remember, step to his side to avoid a punch from his other hand.

Principle: Dividing the muscle/tendon. Your right hand twists his right arm and locks him in position, and your left hand presses his neck down. This technique will not break the neck but it can be used to seal the breath.

Escape and Counter: As with the last technique, step your left leg forward and change your direction to avoid the neck lock. To counter, you can use your left hand to stop his left hand from reaching your neck (Figure 6-40), and then press his wrist down, using both hands to enhance the pain (Figure 6-41).

3. Sou Woh Long Tao (The Arm Holds the Dragon's Head): 手握龍頭
Technique #68: When you have a chance to grab the opponent's right wrist, pull it down and to your right (Figure 6-42), and immediately step your left leg behind his right leg as your left arm wraps his neck (Figure 6-43) and finally holds it down (Figure 6-44). You should hold his right arm

Figure 6-36.

Figure 6-37.

Figure 6-38.

Figure 6-39.

Figure 6-40.

Figure 6-41.

Figure 6-42.

Figure 6-43.

Figure 6-44.

Figure 6-45.

Figure 6-46.

back to lock him in place and hold his neck back until he has lost his balance, otherwise he will still have a root and be able to resist or counterattack you.

Principle: Misplacing the bone and sealing the vein/artery. This technique can be used not only for locking the neck, but also for sealing the oxygen supply to your opponent's brain.

Escape and Counter: Step your left leg forward and change your direction to prevent his left arm from wrapping your neck. To counter, you can use your left hand to stop his left arm from locking your neck (Figure 6-45) and at the same time pull your right hand back while grabbing his wrist and locking his elbow (Figure 6-46).

4. Sou Kow Long Tao (The Hand Seizes the Dragon's Head): 手扣龍頭
Technique #69: If your opponent uses his right hand to strike you, block his attack with your left hand and grab his wrist (Figure 6-47). Then step your right leg to the front of his right leg and at the same time use your right arm to circle his neck (Figure 6-48), and finally use your right

Figure 6-47.

Figure 6-48.

Figure 6-49.

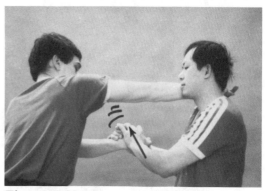

Figure 6-50.

forearm to press up into his neck (Figure 6-49). Remember: step your right leg to his right so that he cannot attack your groin with his left hand. **Principle:** Misplacing the bone, sealing the breath, and sealing the artery. **Escape and Counter:** The first reaction is to keep your opponent at a distance and use your left hand to stop his right arm from circling your neck. To counter, you may use your left hand to lock fingers on his left hand (Figure 6-50) and then press him down (Figure 6-51).

C. Bih Chi (Sealing the Breath) 閉氣

Sealing the breath techniques either seal the windpipe or else strike certain areas to cause the lungs to compress so that air cannot be taken in. You can seal the windpipe by grabbing, squeezing, or even pressing it. To compress the lungs, certain nerves or muscles are struck to cause the muscles around the lungs to contract and compress the lungs. In this chapter we will only discuss sealing the breath through controlling the windpipe. Techniques for compressing the lungs will be discussed in a later chapter.

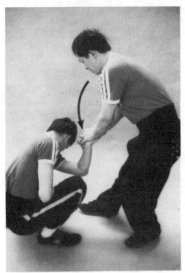

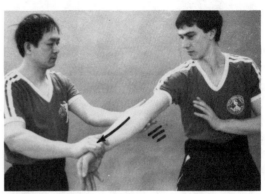

Figure 6-52.

Figure 6-51.

Sealing the Windpipe:

Generally speaking, there are two ways for your hands to reach the opponent's windpipe. For example, when you try to reach the opponent's throat from his right, you may enter from either outside or inside his right arm. Therefore, in order to reach his throat you must first take care of his right arm, because it is threatening to you and it is blocking your attack. There are only a few ways of taking care of the opponent's right arm. We will discuss these ways first, so that we will not need to discuss them for each technique.

1. From Outside of the Opponent's Right Arm:

Your hands can reach the opponent's throat from either above or beneath his right arm. Either way, you must first grab his wrist to limit the arm's mobility. Pull his arm down to open his "sky window" for your entrance (Figure 6-52). Then your right hand will be able to reach his throat either from over his arm (Figure 6-53) or from under his arm, in which case his "sky window" remains open (Figure 6-54). In either case, your left hand should control his elbow so that he cannot counter with that arm or move his body to escape.

It seems pretty easy to reach the opponent's throat. In a real fight, however, it is actually quite difficult. There are two reasons for this. First, once you have pulled the opponent's arm down, his throat is still a good distance away. You must step your right leg forward in order to shorten the range. Unfortunately, once you step, you have shown your intention and have given your opponent a chance to stop your attack. Second, even if one of your hands reaches his throat, it is still not an easy matter to seal his windpipe. You really need two hands to do the job effectively. While one hand reaches the throat, the other should hold the back of his neck to stop him from slipping away. However, if you use both hands, you will probably free both of your opponent's hands, and he will be able to attack you or otherwise put you in a dangerous position. For example, he may be able to reach a hand to your groin or elbow you. You must be aware of all of these possibilities.

The most common defense against an attack to your throat from the right is simply to turn your body to the right and step your left leg to the side and face him (Figure 6-55). This neutralizes your opponent's attack

Figure 6-53.

Figure 6-54.

Figure 6-55.

Figure 6-56.

Figure 6-57.

and his positional advantage, and lets you apply a wrist Chin Na on him.

2. From Inside of the Opponent's Right Arm:

Generally speaking, it is more dangerous to approach your opponent's throat from inside his right arm than from outside. This is because he is able to punch you with his left arm. However, if you approach him correctly and quickly, you might still be able to use the technique effectively. When you intend to reach the opponent's throat from inside his right arm, you must first use your left hand to grab or push away his right arm (Figure 6-56). This gives you an opportunity to step your right leg to his right and move your right hand to his throat (Figure 6-57). Remember: **WHEN YOU APPROACH YOUR OPPONENT'S RIGHT SIDE, STEP IN WITH YOUR RIGHT LEG TO PROTECT YOUR GROIN,** otherwise he can kick you with his right knee.

When your opponent approaches you from your right side, your defense is the same whether he is coming from inside or outside of your arm: step your left leg around and face him.

Technique #70: When your opponent punches you with his right hand, intercept with your left hand and pull in and lock his arm with your right hand (Figure 6-58). Immediately step to the side and lock his right elbow (Figure 6-59). Finally, place your right hand on his throat while your left is still controlling him (Figure 6-60).

Figure 6-58.

Figure 6-59.

Figure 6-60.

Figure 6-61.

Figure 6-62.

Figure 6-63.

Technique #71: If you are behind him and your left arm is around his throat, push his head forward with your right hand while holding your right arm with your left hand to seal his breath (Figure 6-61).

Technique #72: Use your right hand to grab the opponent's throat while your left hand holds the back of his neck to immobilize his head (Figure 6-62). When you use this technique, make him lean backward so that his balance is destroyed. Then he will have a hard time resisting you or striking you with his elbow.

Technique #73: Once your right arm has locked the opponent's throat from behind, slide your left arm under his left armpit and lock his left arm, and pull him to the side to destroy his balance (Figure 6-63).

Technique #74: This technique is used only when your opponent is on the floor. Simply press down on his throat with your right forearm while pulling his clothes to the side with your left hand (Figure 6-64).

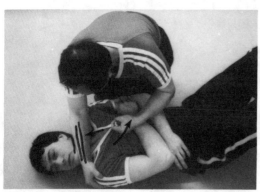

Figure 6-64.

Figure 6-65.

Technique #75: Once you have pulled your opponent's right arm down, slip your left arm over it and underneath his throat. Move your right arm over his neck and clasp hands (Figure 6-65), then squeeze your arms together to choke him. Make sure to keep your opponent leaning forward so that he cannot counterattack.

Technique #76: Once you have pulled your opponent's right arm down, grab his hair with your right hand and pull his head down. Immediately use your left arm to lock his throat with the help of your right hand (Figure 6-66).

Technique #77: Once your right arm has reached the opponent's throat, step to his rear and use your left arm to lock his left arm. Press his head forward with your left hand to seal the breath (Figure 6-67).

D. Duann Mie (Sealing the Vein/Artery) 斷脈

As mentioned before, sealing the vein/artery refers to the techniques for stopping the oxygen supply to the brain. When the brain is deprived of oxygen for over five seconds, unconsciousness or even death will result. There are two major arteries, one on either side of the neck, which supply oxygen to the brain.

Arteries are most commonly sealed by pressing or striking. When pressing techniques are used, you usually squeeze both sides of the neck at the same time while your opponent is locked in a controlled position. Most pressing techniques are similar to those used to seal the windpipe or lock the neck. The only thing you have to do is to change the sealing location to the sides of the neck instead of the throat. You will find that a number of the techniques for sealing the windpipe and locking the neck also seal the arteries at the same time. These techniques will not be discussed further here. In this section we will discuss only those techniques which use a strike or a point press for the sealing. However, when you use sealing the artery techniques, you must know one important thing. **WHEN THE ARTERY IS SEALED, IT MAY REMAIN SEALED EVEN AFTER YOU RELEASE THE PRESSURE. THIS WILL USUALLY CAUSE DEATH BECAUSE YOU HAVE DEPRIVED THE BRAIN OF OXYGEN.** This is because when the side of the neck is struck or pressed, the muscles there will

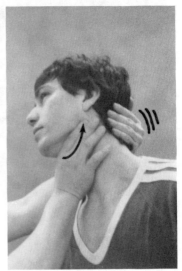

Figure 6-66.   Figure 6-67.   Figure 6-68.

contract and tighten up in the same way that leg muscles sometimes cramp up during swimming. Therefore, think twice before you use these techniques. In Chapter 11 we will discuss one of the ways to release the tightened muscles so that a person may recover from a sealing the artery technique.

Sealing the Artery by Striking and Cavity Pressing:
Technique #78: When you have a chance to reach the opponent's throat either from outside or inside of his arm, use your thumb and index finger to press the cavities under the ears where the arteries are located (Figure 6-68). When you do this you should also lock the back of his neck or head with your left hand and pull forward to increase the pressure.

Technique #79: When you have a chance to grab the opponent's hand or wrist, you can use elbow Chin Na to immobilize him and then seal one of his neck arteries from the rear with your thumb (Figure 6-69). This technique will only cut off half of the oxygen supply to his brain, but that will be enough to make him lose his balance or even pass out.

Technique #80: When you have a chance to strike the side of your opponent's neck, use a knife-hand to strike either one side (Figure 6-70) or both sides (Figure 6-71). This will cause the muscles in the side of the neck to contract and seal the artery.

6-4. Waist Chin Na Techniques
Before we discuss waist Chin Na, let us first look at the structure of the waist. The major support of the waist is the spine, which is connected to the pelvis at the sacrum, and to the head at the first cervical vertebra (Figure 6-72). In front of the spine are the small and large intestines. Around the organs are layers of muscles which run from both inside and outside of the ribs down (Figure 6-73). These muscles protect your organs, yet also give you the ability to bend and twist.

Generally speaking, it is pretty hard to divide the muscles/tendons in the waist area. However, since many of the muscles in the waist extend upward to the vicinity of the organs inside the ribs, it is possible to strike muscles in the waist and use their contraction to shock organs in a different area. For example, when the stomach area is struck, the muscle

Figure 6-69.

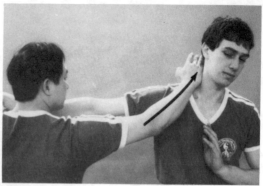

Figure 6-70.

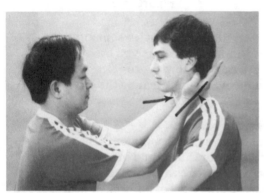

Figure 6-71.

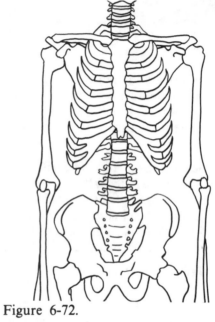

Figure 6-72.

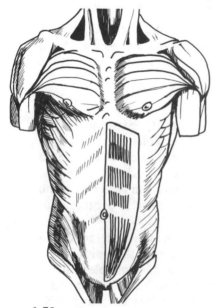

Figure 6-73.

Figure 6-74.   Figure 6-75.

contraction can cause the lungs to compress so they cannot take in air.

Since the waist is strong and hard to reach, not too many locking or breaking Chin Na techniques have been developed. In order to lock or break the spine at the waist, you have to bend the opponent backward and misplace the bones. In this section we will introduce only a few of the available waist Chin Na.

Waist Chin Na:
1. Sou Baw Da Shyong (Arms Embrace the Large Bear): 手抱大熊
Technique #81: Frequently while fighting or wrestling you will have the opportunity to hold your opponent's waist. When you do, hold it tight and bend forward (Figure 6-74). You must bend forward until your opponent loses his balance, otherwise he will be able to knee you.
Principle: Misplacing the bones. It is easier for you to bend forward than it is for your opponent to bend backward, so you will cause him considerable pain.
Escape and Counter: Once you sense the embrace, twist your body to the side immediately before his arms lock your waist. To counter, you can strike him in both temples with your hands. Alternatively, you can use both hands to hold his head and at the same time hop up and use your knee to kick his groin or stomach.

2. Bai Gang Meeng Hwu (Carry a Fierce Tiger on your Back) 背扛猛虎
Technique #82: When you can put one arm around your opponent's neck from the rear, turn your back to him and pull him backwards, while simultaneously pulling one of his legs to bend his spine (Figure 6-75). This technique can be used to break his spine.
Principle: Misplacing the bone. You will need a lot of muscle to do the job, so if you are weak and smaller than your opponent, this technique is not practical.
Escape and Counter: Right before your neck is circled, you should twist your body and neck to change the angle and neutralize the attack. Once you are facing your opponent, if you see that he is big and powerful and intends to do you serious harm, do not hesitate to attack his eyes and groin. No matter how big the opponent is, these two spots are always vulnerable.

Figure 6-76.

3. Hai Bao Shen Iau (Seal Stretches its Body) 海豹伸腰

Technique #83: Whenever your opponent is on the floor with his face down, lock his legs with one hand and his neck with the other, and pull them together while pressing his back with your knee (Figure 6-76).

Principle: Misplacing the bone.

Escape and Counter: Whenever you are on the ground, always face up so you can defend yourself with all your hands and legs.

CHAPTER 7
LEG CHIN NA

7-1. Introduction

Chin Na is also used on the legs, although there are not as many techniques available as there are for the arms. In the first place, the legs are harder to reach than the hands and arms. Secondly, the leg is much stronger than the arm, and so it is harder to control. Thirdly, the toes are shorter than the fingers, and they are commonly protected by shoes, so there is no toe Chin Na.

Generally speaking, there are only two joints in the leg which are commonly used for Chin Na control: the ankle and the knee. You can apply Chin Na techniques with either your legs or your hands, though the number using the legs is limited. Most of the time, the hands are much more versatile and useful than the legs. Normally, it is almost impossible to reach your opponent's legs and apply a Chin Na while he is in a stable stance. However, there are some cases when an opportunity will present itself, for example, when your opponent kicks. You will then have a good chance to grab his foot and apply Chin Na on it. In order to use a leg Chin Na against a kick, you must first know how to intercept the kick. In Chapter 10 we will introduce some of the leg intercepting techniques used for Chin Na applications. Another opportunity for leg Chin Na occurs when your opponent is on the floor, or when you make him fall. You then may have a chance to control his legs.

Generally speaking, your ankles and knees are structured similarly to your wrists and elbows. The principles of application are therefore the same as those for the wrist and elbow. For example, the major principle of the Chin Na used on the ankle is dividing the muscle/tendon, while at the knee it is misplacing the bone. For this reason we will not go over the structure of the ankle and knee.

Techniques for making the opponent fall greatly reduce his fighting capability, and so they are a major part of the training in ground Chin Na and Chinese wrestling. We will introduce some of these techniques first, and then we will introduce some of the common leg Chin Na techniques. To make the opponent fall, you usually must first intercept his attack or set him up in a position advantageous to you. In Chapter 10 we will introduce some of the common intercepting techniques.

Figure 7-1.   Figure 7-2.   Figure 7-3.

7-2. Leg Chin Na Techniques
Techniques to Make the Opponent Fall:

In order to make your opponent fall, you must first intercept his arm and push him down either from inside or outside of his arm. Taking him down from inside is called internal upsetting while taking him down from outside his arm is called external upsetting.

A. Internal Upsetting:

Technique #84: In this technique, assume you have intercepted your opponent's right hand punch. Step your left leg behind the opponent's right leg and at the same time use your right hand to grab and pull his right leg. While you are doing this, your left hand should be controlling his left arm, and should be pressing his chest in the area of his armpit (Figure 7-1). Then push your left hand forward while pulling your right hand backward to upset him (Figure 7-2).

Technique #85: This technique is similar to the last technique except that this time you use both of your hands to pull his right root (Figure 7-3), and at the same time use your left shoulder to bounce him off balance (Figure 7-4).

Technique #86: In this technique, you first intercept the opponent's right hand punch with your left hand and push it away, which will give you a chance to step your right leg behind his right leg, and also allow you to use your right hand to grab his right ankle (Figure 7-5). Then pull your right hand up while pulling your left hand down to destroy his balance (Figure 7-6).

Technique #87: Whenever you have the chance, for example when your opponent intends to grab your chest, bow your body down and at the same time step your right leg forward and grab both of his leg (Figure 7-7). Immediately pull both hands up while bouncing him with your shoulder (Figure 7-8).

Technique #88: After you have intercepted your opponent's punch, step your left leg behind his right leg and at the same time place your left arm in front of his neck (Figure 7-9). Immediately push him backward with your left arm while your left thigh bounces his right thigh up and forward

Figure 7-4.

Figure 7-5.

Figure 7-6.

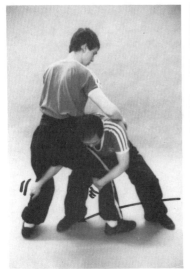

Figure 7-7.

Figure 7-8.

Figure 7-9.

(Figure 7-10).

Technique #89: In this technique, use your left hand to intercept your opponent's right punch and grab his arm. Then push his right arm to the side while stepping your right leg in front of his right leg, and place your right arm behind his chest (Figure 7-11). Immediately push your left hand forward, push your right hand backward, and at the same time use your right thigh to bounce his right thigh and knock him off balance (Figure 7-12).

Technique #90: In this technique you also use your left hand to grab and intercept the opponent's right punch. Then you step your right leg behind his right leg while placing your right hand around his neck (Figure 7-13). Immediately push your right arm forward and bounce your right thigh backward to pull his right root (Figure 7-14).

B. External Upsetting:
Technique #91: After you have intercepted your opponent's right punch

Figure 7-10.

Figure 7-11.

Figure 7-12.

Figure 7-13.

Figure 7-14.

Figure 7-15.

with your right hand, step your right leg forward and use both of your hands to grab his right leg (Figure 7-15). Pull his right leg up while using your shoulder to bounce his body off balance (Figure 7-16).

Technique #92: Once you have intercepted the opponent's right punch from outside of his arm, step your left leg behind his right leg, place his right arm on your right shoulder with his palm up, and at the same time use your left hand to hold his right thigh (Figure 7-17). Lift his right leg with your left arm while also using your shoulder to bounce backward to make him lose his balance (Figure 7-18).

Technique #93: After you have intercepted the opponent's right punch, pull his right hand down and at the same time step your left leg behind his right leg and place your left arm against his chest (Figure 7-19). Press backward with your left arm while using your left thigh to bounce forward against his right thigh (Figure 7-20). This will make him fall instantly.

Figure 7-16.

Figure 7-17.

Figure 7-18.

Figure 7-19.

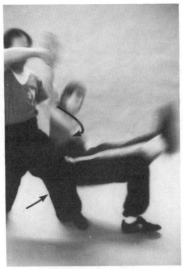
Figure 7-20.

Figure 7-21.

Technique #94: In this technique, first use your right arm to intercept the opponent's right punch from outside of his arm (Figure 7-21). Then circle your arm to his elbow and grab his right wrist with your left hand while stepping your right leg behind his right leg (Figure 7-22). Finally, pull forward with both hands while sliding your right leg backward to upset him (Figure 7-23).

Technique #95: This time, after you have intercepted the punch, step your left leg behind his right leg while placing your left arm around his neck (Figure 7-24). Your left knee should be touching the back of his right knee. Push his neck backward while bouncing your left thigh forward to upset his balance (Figure 7-25).

Technique #96: This technique is similar to several of the previous techniques. Place the opponent's right arm on your right shoulder with his palm facing up while your left leg is behind him and your left arm is around his body (Figure 7-26). Bounce your shoulder backward and your left thigh forward against his right thigh to make him fall (Figure 7-27).

Figure 7-22.

Figure 7-23.

Figure 7-24.

Figure 7-25.

Figure 7-26.

Figure 7-27.

Technique #97: After you have intercepted and grabbed your opponent's right wrist, pull it down and at the same time place your left leg against his abdomen (Figure 7-28). Then slide your body down to the floor while placing your right leg behind both of his legs (Figure 7-29). Finally, press your left leg backward while pushing your right leg forward to make him fall (Figure 7-30).

C. Circling:

Technique #98: Once you have locked the opponent's wrist and elbow with both hands (Figure 7-31), step your right leg to your rear to set up the position (Figure 7-32). Finally, keeping pressure on his elbow with your forearm, sit back on your rear leg and circle him to the floor, pulling him with both hands (Figure 7-33).

D. Against a Kick:

Technique #99: After you have intercepted a right kick, step your left leg behind his left leg and place your left arm against his chest (Figure 7-34).

Figure 7-28.

Figure 7-29.

Figure 7-30.

Figure 7-31.

Figure 7-32.

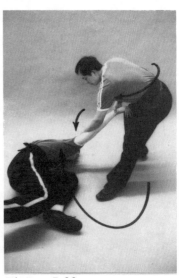

Figure 7-33.

Then push your left hand backward while sliding your left leg forward to make him fall (Figure 7-35).

The techniques introduced above are only some of the techniques which you can use to make the opponent fall. You should continue your research or refer to some of the ground fighting styles to increase your knowledge. From the above discussion, it seems easy to apply these techniques to an opponent. In fact, in a real fight it is not so easy at all. To use these techniques effectively requires a great deal of practice, and must know how to set the opponent up, otherwise all of the above techniques are good only for showing off and not for fighting.

Leg Chin Na:
A. Using a Leg to Apply Leg Chin Na:
Technique #100: In this and the next technique you use your leg to lock and press the opponent's front knee. If your opponent's right toes are too much inward, use your left leg to hook behind his right ankle (Figure 7-

Figure 7-34.

Figure 7-35.

Figure 7-36.

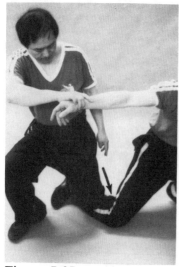

Figure 7-37.

Figure 7-38.

Figure 7-39.

36), and press your knee down against his knee to force him down (Figure 7-37). If you press your knee in the right angle you might be able to break his knee joint.

Technique #101: However, if you find that your opponent's toes are too much outward, then you have a chance to use this technique. Following the same principle as the previous technique, use your right leg to hook his right ankle (Figure 7-38), and press his shin to the side to make him fall (Figure 7-39).

Technique #102: This technique is used when you are on the ground. You can use your right leg to hook his ankle and at the same time use your left leg to kick or press his knee cap (Figure 7-40). If you apply this technique with the right angle and right power, you may very easily dislocate his kneecap.

Figure 7-40.

Figure 7-41.

Figure 7-42.

B. Leg Chin Na on a Downed Opponent:

Technique #103: If your opponent falls to the ground and tries to kick you, you might have a chance to catch his leg. If this happens, lock his leg with your arm and press up against his calf with your forearm (Figure 7-41). Pressing the muscle this way is very painful.

Technique #104: When you opponent falls and you have a chance to catch his leg, sit on his stomach and twist his ankle clockwise with both hands (Figure 7-42).

Technique #105: This technique is the same as the last one except that here you twist his ankle in the other direction (Figure 7-43).

Technique #106: Sometimes you will find that it is too dangerous for you to sit on his stomach since he might still be able to punch you or kick your with his other leg. In this case, twist his leg to make him turn over first and then sit on his hip and twist his ankle clockwise (Figure 7-44) or counterclockwise (Figure 7-45).

C. Leg Chin Na Against Kicks:

Technique #107: In order to apply a leg Chin Na against a kick, you must first learn how to intercept a kick and catch his leg. Refer to Chapter 10 for some of these techniques. Once you have caught his leg, apply pressure to his toes to twist his ankle and cause pain (Figure 7-46).
Principle: Dividing the Muscle/Tendon.
Escape: Once you have found that your leg is grabbed, before your leg is locked in place, immediately turn your body and bend your knee (Figure 7-47). Then kick your leg backward toward his body and roll away (Figure 7-48).

Technique #108: This technique is similar to the last one except that you twist his ankle to the other side (Figure 7-49).
Principle: Misplacing the Bones. If your opponent uses this technique to lock your ankle, you will not be able to use the escape technique shown above.

Figure 7-43.

Figure 7-44.

Figure 7-45.

Figure 7-46.

Figure 7-47.

Figure 7-48.

Figure 7-49.

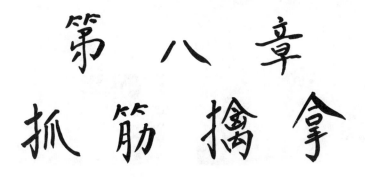

CHAPTER 8
MUSCLE GRABBING
CHIN NA

8-1. Introduction

Jua Jin (grabbing the muscle/tendon) Chin Na is used frequently in certain Chinese martial styles, especially those which rely heavily on the hands and fingers, such as eagle, crane, and tiger styles. The principle of grabbing the muscle/tendon Chin Na is very simple, and the techniques are not very deep or complicated. However, when this Chin Na is used together with cavity press, the techniques become deeper and more complicated.

The simplest forms of grabbing the muscle/tendon Chin Na use the fingers to grab a group of muscle fibers and either pull them from their original position or tear them off the bone they are attached to. Usually the muscles or tendons which are grabbed are in the joint areas. Grabbing muscles/tendons causes pain. When extreme pain is caused, the Chi channels which pass through the joint are disturbed. When the pain is strong enough, the Chi disturbance can be significant and can damage the related organs. However, usually before this point is reached, your brain has already given the order to let you pass out.

Because many cavities are located near the joints, very often when a grabbing the muscle/tendon Chin Na is used, cavity press is also used simultaneously. When this happens, not only are the muscles in the joint controlled, but the Chi circulation is also disturbed immediately. Usually the simultaneous use of cavity press can make the opponent pass out much more easily or make his limb numb. There are also some vital cavities located in the joint areas, for example in the armpit. When these cavities are pressed accurately and with the right power and timing, death can result.

Although cavity press is effective and potent, it requires a great deal of knowledge and training to make it work. For example, Chi and Jing are required so that the power can penetrate the right depth to the Chi

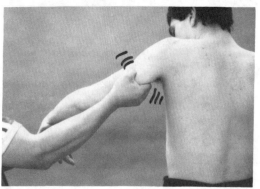
Figure 8-1.

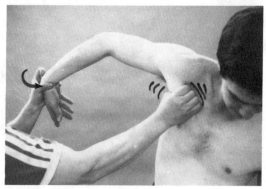
Figure 8-2.

channel. For a detailed discussion of Chi and Jing, please refer to the author's book: *Advanced Yang Style Tai Chi Chuan—Tai Chi Theory and Jing, Vol. 1.*

Normally it is very easy to defend against a grabbing Chin Na, as long as you remain calm and have strong muscles. If you have Chi Kung training, it is even harder for the attacker to control you by grabbing your muscles. If someone does try to grab your muscles/tendons, remain calm, concentrate on the muscles being grabbed, and tense them up. When you concentrate, your Chi will support the muscles you are concentrating on and energize them, which will usually make the muscle fibers expand and behave as if they were strongly inflated with air. This muscle expansion will generate a shield to keep the opponent's power from reaching into your Chi channels or nearby cavities and affecting your Chi circulation. Consequently, you will not feel as much pain as you would if you hadn't tensed up your muscles. This is a basic external way of Chinese Iron Shirt or Golden Bell Cover training. In such training you must also train to lead your Chi to support the muscles and bounce the opponent's power back to him. Because of the depth and complication of such training, we will not go into it further here.

8-2. Muscle Grabbing Techniques

Technique #109: Grabbing and squeezing the upper part of the triceps (Figure 8-1) generates pain and numbness. When you use this grabbing Chin Na your other hand should grab the opponent's wrist to prevent him from moving, and you should stand behind him to avoid an attack from his other hand.

Technique #110: Grabbing and pulling the muscles in the front of the armpit generates numbness in the shoulder area (Figure 8-2). If the pulling and squeezing power is strong enough, this grabbing Chin Na can cause the lung to compress and seal the breath. When you use this Chin Na you should also control his wrist with your other hand and stand at his side to keep away from any attack from his other hand.

Technique #111: Grabbing and squeezing the muscles in the back of the armpit (Figure 8-3) causes numbness in the shoulder area. If strong power is applied, the pain can make the opponent pass out. When you use this technique, use your other hand to control his wrist and stand behind him to avoid any further attack.

Technique #112: There is a cavity called Shoulder Well (Jianjing) located on the big muscles running to the side and back of the neck. When this

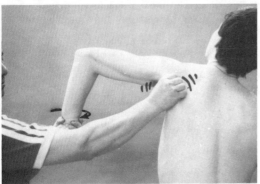

Figure 8-3.

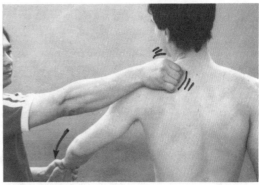

Figure 8-4.

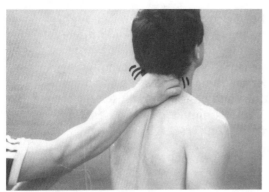

Figure 8-5.

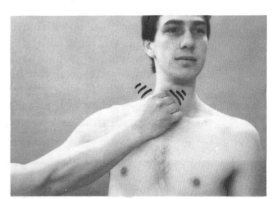

Figure 8-6.

area is grabbed and squeezed (Figure 8-4), it can affect the Chi circulation and generate extreme pain. If the pain is strong enough, it will shock the brain and make you pass out. When you use this technique, you should grab his wrist with your other hand and stand behind him so he cannot attack you.

Technique #113: The muscles on the back of the neck are directly related to the brain. Striking or grabbing these muscles can usually make the opponent pass out (Figure 8-5).

Technique #114: When the muscles on the side of the throat are grabbed and squeezed (Figure 8-6), extreme pain is generated. If this pain is significant, it can cause the muscles around the neck to contract and cut off the oxygen supply to the brain. This is an example of sealing the vein/artery.

Technique #115: Grabbing the muscles on either side of the waist (Figure 8-7) can cause extreme pain and make the opponent pass out. Since these two spots are so close to the liver and spleen, serious pain can cause the liver to rupture and the spleen to malfunction, usually causing death.

Technique #116: In this technique you don't grab muscles, instead you grab bones—the clavicles in the upper chest (Figure 8-8). Grabbing and squeezing these bones causes extreme pain and immobilizes upper body movement. Significant pain will cause unconsciousness.

To conclude this short chapter, you must first understand that in order to make the techniques work you need considerable finger grabbing

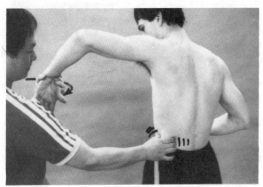

Figure 8-7.   Figure 8-8.

strength. In addition, you also need to be able to concentrate well enough so that you can generate sufficient Chi to overwhelm the Chi and muscle tension which your opponent will use against your grab. In this chapter we have only introduced the basic principles and some examples of grabbing Chin Na. There are many other grabbing Chin Na which attack smaller muscles, such as the ankle tendons and elbow joint muscles, but these are usually not as effective as the techniques discussed in this chapter. We will leave these other areas to your research.

CHAPTER 9
CAVITY PRESS

9-1. Introduction

Cavity press in Chinese martial arts generally includes two different categories: "Tien Hsueh" (cavity press) and "Tien Shiee" (blood press). Literally Tien Hsueh (cavity press) can be translated as "Pointing Cavity" and Tien Shiee as "Pointing Blood". Pointing has the meaning of aiming at a tiny spot, penetrating to a depth, and pressing. Frequently it will also mean striking. That is why these techniques are also called "Da Hsueh" (Strike Cavity) or "Da Shiee" (Strike Blood). Striking a cavity affects the Chi circulation, and striking the blood strikes blood vessels to rupture them. Frequently, the place which is effective for blood striking is also the same spot for Chi striking, for example the temple.

The human body has twelve Chi channels which are related to the internal organs, and an additional eight major vessels which also circulate Chi in the body. There are more than seven hundred acupuncture cavities, most of them along these channels and vessels. The majority of these cavities can be treated by acupuncture needles. When a needle reaches a cavity it can affect the Chi circulation in the channel, either stimulating or sedating it, and adjust the Chi's Yin and Yang balance, thus curing illness.

Overstimulation of Chi in a cavity can damage the corresponding organ. Among all these cavities are about 108 through which the Chi can be overstimulated by striking or pressing with the fingers. Of these 108 cavities, 72 can be used to destroy the opponent's fighting ability by rendering him unconscious or numbing parts of his body, and 36 cavities can be used to kill or seriously injure him. Pressing or hitting these cavities with the proper power can also be used to adjust and regulate the Chi, and this is commonly used in acupressure massage. However, vigorous stimulation of vital cavities, either through pressing or striking, can either send a flood of Chi to shock the organ, or seal the Chi circulation to the organ and make it malfunction because of insufficient Chi.

In order to make the attack effective, you must also understand how the Chi flow in the body changes according to the season and the time of day. The relation of time and Chi flow is called "Tzu Wuu Lieu Ju". Tzu means midnight and Wuu means midday, Lieu means flow and Ju means to direct or to pour. Tzu Wuu Lieu Ju is the schedule describing the time and location of the major Chi flow in the body. In addition, you must have special training in Chi, Jing, and specific striking techniques. The basic requirements of cavity press are accurate striking and correct timing. Jing is the key to penetrating power and effective strikes. An advanced martial artist with the special Chi training can overflow his Chi to the opponent's body with just a touch to a cavity and shock the opponent's organs. However, it is no longer easy to find a martial artist who has reached this level.

In a fight, blood press is used mainly to affect the blood circulation by either reducing the blood supply or even rupturing a blood vessel. Some Chinese martial artists include organ striking among the techniques of blood striking. When organs such as the heart, liver, or kidneys are struck directly, the muscles around the organs contract. This causes a sudden diminishing of the blood supply which will shock some organs such as the heart, or even rupture organs such as the liver or kidney.

From the above discussion you can see that cavity press is one of the highest levels of technique which a martial artist can reach. It requires not only a deep and wide knowledge of martial techniques, human anatomy, and Chi circulation, but also long and in-depth training in the techniques. It is impossible to discuss this subject in a chapter. To learn cavity press requires long study with a qualified and experienced master. Such a person is hard to find. With firearms so universally available, few people feel the need to spend years learning the art, and it is gradually disappearing. Even if a book on cavity press were written, it would of necessity be limited in scope, since many techniques can only be learned through feeling and sensing. In this chapter we will introduce only some typical examples of techniques from the different categories of cavity press. Instead of trying to teach cavity press from a book, we will only introduce the reader to the art.

To defend against a cavity press attack, you usually need to have Chi Kung training, either Wai Dan (External Elixir), or Nei Dan (Internal Elixir). This training will give you the ability to either generate Chi in parts of your body so that they can resist an attack, or else generate it in the Dan Tien and lead this Chi to the area being attacked. This Chi will energize the muscles so that they can resist the outside attack effectively. Chi Kung can also be used to shield your cavities from attack. Such training is called "Tiee Buh Shan" (Iron Shirt) or "Jin Jong Jaw" (Golden Bell Cover). If you are interested in Chi Kung, you should refer to the author's book *Chi Kung—Health and Martial Arts*.

9-2. Cavity Press Techniques
A. Ya Hsueh Far (Cavity Pressing Method) 壓穴法

The cavity pressing method uses the fingers to press the opponent's cavities to seal the Chi circulation. This either causes numbness in a part of his body, or else shocks an organ, which usually causes the opponent to pass out before the organ is damaged. Most of the cavities which cause numbness are located in the limbs, while the cavities which cause your opponent to pass out are located both on the body and the limbs. The most important factors in a successful cavity press are your Yi (mind, will) and Chi, for they direct your power into the cavities themselves. This allows you to affect your opponent's Chi directly, rather than indirectly

Figure 9-1.

Figure 9-2.

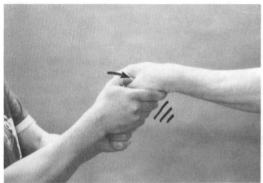

Figure 9-3.

Figure 9-4.

by affecting the muscles around the channels. Most of the time, if you only use muscle when applying these techniques, you will only cause pain, and no serious damage. We will now show the location of some of the cavities, and some of the common way of pressing.

Technique #117: There are six Chi channels which extend to the ends of the fingers, and each has a vulnerable cavity. The little finger has one channel on either side (Heart, Shaochong cavity; Small Intestine, Shaoze cavity), the other four fingers have one each (Thumb: Lung Channel, Shaoshang; Second Finger: Large Intestine, Shangyang; Middle Finger: Pericardium, Zhong-chong; Ring Finger: Triple-Burner, Guanchong). Pinching the side of the finger tip (Figure 9-1) causes serious pain and affects the Chi circulation. If this pain is significant, it can make you pass out. Sometimes the top of the nail is squeezed (Figure 9-2), which will also affect the Chi and the nerves in that area, and cause the same results.

Technique #118: Hegu or Fukou is a cavity located in the pit between the forefinger and the thumb. This cavity is on the Large Intestine Channel. Pressing this area (Figure 9-3) can cause numbness if minor pain is caused. However, if serious pain is generated it can affect the organ and make the opponent pass out.

Technique #119: The Hand-Zhongshu cavity is on the Sanjiao or Triple-Burner Channel. Pressing this cavity (Figures 9-4 and 9-5) can cause pain or numbness, or can even shock the brain and make the opponent pass out.

Figure 9-5.

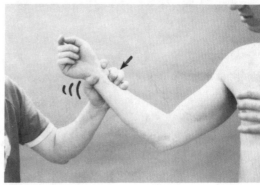

Figure 9-6.

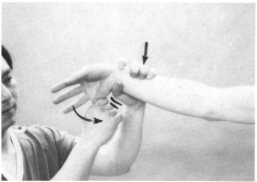

Figure 9-7.

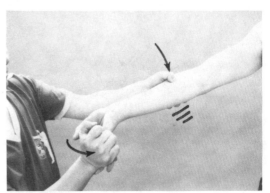

Figure 9-8.

Technique #120: The Neiguan or Wanmei cavity is located on the inside of the forearm near the wrist. It is on the Pericardium Channel, which passes through the area of the lung. Pressing this cavity with the right power and timing (Figure 9-6) can cause the lung to contract and make the opponent faint. This cavity press is used frequently in Chin Na techniques which include a wrist grab, because it can immobilize the opponent's arm (Figure 9-7).

Technique #121: The Kongzui cavity is located on the inside of the forearm, on the Lung Channel. Pressing this cavity hard (Figure 9-8) can cause the lung to contract so that the opponent passes out. When is is pressed with lesser power, it can cause pain and numbness in the arm.

Technique #122: The Chize cavity is located on the inside of the arm near the elbow, on the Lung Channel. Pressing this cavity (Figure 9-9) can cause pain and numbness or even unconsciousness.

Technique #123: The Quchi cavity is located on the side of the elbow, on the Large Intestine Channel. Pressing this cavity (Figure 9-10) causes pain and numbness.

Technique #124: The Shaohai cavity is located in the funny bone area. It is on the Heart Channel. Pressing this cavity (Figure 9-11) can cause the whole arm to go numb. Pressing with significant power can cause a heart attack.

Technique #125: The Qingling cavity is located on the inside of the upper arm, on the Heart Channel. Pressing this cavity (Figure 9-12) can cause numbness in the arm or even a heart attack.

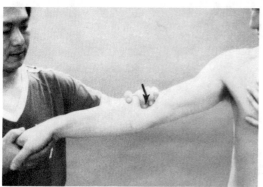
Figure 9-9.

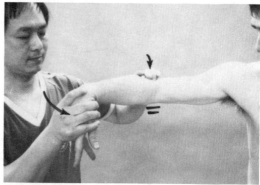
Figure 9-10.

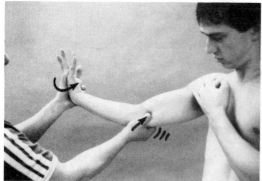
Figure 9-11.

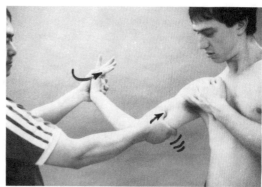
Figure 9-12.

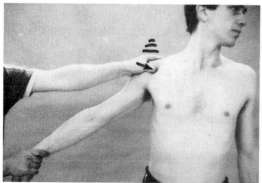
Figure 9-13.

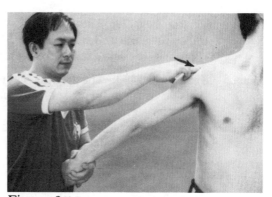
Figure 9-14.

Technique #126: The front of the shoulder joint can also be attacked. The Heart Channel passes through here. Striking or pressing this spot (Figure 9-13) can cause the arm to go numb and also affect the Chi circulation in the Heart Channel.

Technique #127: The Jianyu cavity is located on the top of the shoulder joint, on the Large Intestine Channel. Pressing or striking this cavity (Figure 9-14) can cause numbness in the arm.

Technique #128: The Qihu cavity is located on the upper side of the chest, on the Stomach Channel. Qihu means "the air door". Because this channel passes near the lung, pressing or striking it (Figure 9-15) will agitate the lungs and cause coughing. A serious attack can seal the breath.

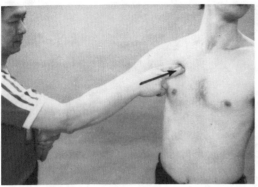

Figure 9-15.

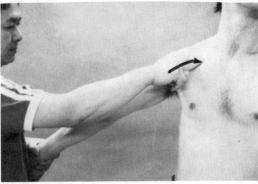

Figure 9-16.

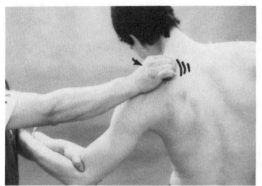

Figure 9-17.

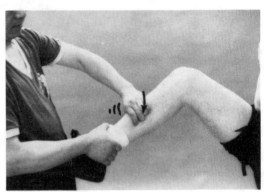

Figure 9-18.

Technique #129: The Quepen cavity is located only a few inches above the Qihu cavity and is also on the Stomach Channel. Attacking this cavity (Figure 9-16) can generate the same results as with the Qihu cavity.

Technique #130: The Jianjing cavity or shoulder well cavity is located on the side of the upper back. This cavity is on the Gall Bladder Channel. Striking or pressing this cavity (Figure 9-17) can cause the shoulder to become numb. A serious attack can shock the opponent's brain with pain, and may cause unconsciousness.

Technique #131: The Lougu cavity is located on the inside of the shin, on the Spleen Channel. Pressing or kicking this cavity (Figure 9-18) can cause the leg to go numb.

Technique #132: The Xuehai cavity is located on the inside of the thigh near the knee. This cavity also is on the Spleen Channel. Kicking or pressing this cavity (Figure 9-19) can cause numbness in the leg.

B. Da Hsueh Far (Cavity Striking Method) 打穴法
1. Striking Yin-Yang Connections:
   There are a few cavities in which the Chi changes between Yin and Yang channels. When these cavities are attacked with the right timing and power, the Yin and Yang exchange is affected, usually causing instant death.

Technique #133: Baihui means "hundred meeting point". It is also called Tien Ling Gai, which means Heavenly Spirit Cover. It is a major Chi center, and it is one of the places where the Yin and Yang exchange. This

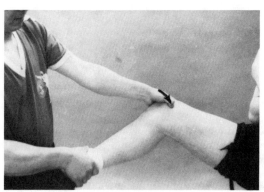

Figure 9-19.

Figure 9-20.

cavity belongs to the Du Mie (Governing Vessel) and is directly related to the brain. Striking this spot at the right time (Figure 9-20) can cause instant death.

Technique #134: The other cavity where Yin and Yang exchange is called Huiyin and means Meeting of the Yin. This cavity is also called Haidi, which means Sea Bottom. It is located about one inch behind the groin and is on the Ren Mie (Conception vessel). Striking this cavity at the right time (Figure 9-21) can affect the Chi exchange from Yin to Yang, and may cause death within 24 hours.

2. Striking Cavities

Among the eight Chi vessels and twelve Chi channels, there are more than 80 cavities which can cause numbness, unconsciousness, or even death when struck. We will only introduce some of these cavities here. The time and the techniques of striking will not be discussed. Some of the cavities, even though they are listed as causing numbness or unconsciousness when struck, might still cause death or serious injury. Therefore, **DO NOT ATTEMPT TO EXPERIMENT WITH THESE CAVITIES—IT IS EXTREMELY DANGEROUS.**

a. Vital Cavities:

Technique #135: The Lingtai cavity is located between the sixth and seventh thoracic vertabrae. Lingtai means Spiritual Station in Chinese. This is because the Chinese believe that the heart is your spiritual power center. The Lingtai cavity is located directly opposite the heart, and is on the Du Mie (Governing vessel). Striking this cavity (Figure 9-22) affects the Chi circulation, and will cause the muscles around the heart to contract, possibly resulting in a heart attack.

Technique #136: Jiquan means the Extreme Spring and is located in the armpit. This cavity is on the Heart Channel, and while it is located deep inside the body, it is very vulnerable. Striking this cavity (Figure 9-23) can cause a heart attack in the same way that the funny bone can cause the arm to go numb when struck.

Technique #137: Dan Tien means the "Field of Elixir". It is also called Qihai, which means "Sea of Chi". It is the most important spot in your

Figure 9-21.

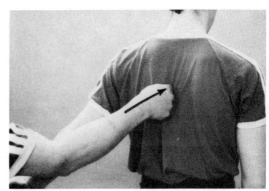

Figure 9-22.

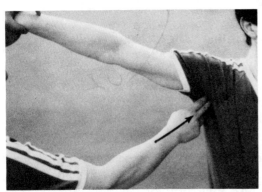

Figure 9-23.

Figure 9-24.

Chi circulation. This is the spot where Chi is generated, and it is important in keeping your internal energy circulation strong and vigorous. When this spot is struck and injured (Figure 9-24), the "Chi factory" is destroyed and the person will die.

b. Cavities Causing Unconsciousness (Excluding Bih Chi):
Technique #138: Yamen means "Dumb Door" and is located on the back of the neck. When an acupuncture needle enters this cavity, it can control your larynx and stop you from talking. On the sides of this cavity are two large muscles which pass into the skull. Striking either this cavity or these two muscles (Figure 9-25) will shock the brain, causing unconsciousness.

Technique #139: Tianzhu means the "Heaven Post" and is located on the Bladder Channel, on the sides of the back of the neck. As mentioned above, there are two muscles which pass through the back of the neck to support the head (the "Heaven"). When this cavity is attacked or one of the muscles struck (Figure 9-26), one side of the brain will be shocked, causing unconsciousness.

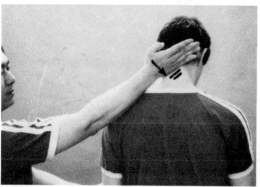

Figure 9-25.

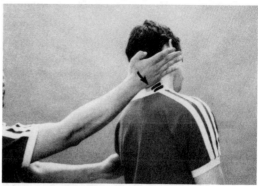

Figure 9-26.

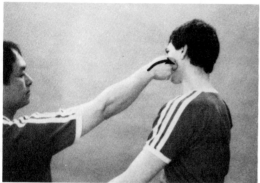

Figure 9-27.

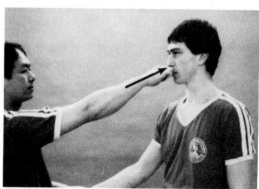

Figure 9-28.

Technique #140: The Jiache or Yasha cavity is located on the side of the jaw. This cavity is on the Stomach Channel. Striking this cavity will cause the opponent to collapse (Figure 9-27). A strong attack may cause death.

Technique #141: The Renzhong or Suigao cavity is located under the nose. It is on the Du Mie. Striking this cavity can cause unconsciousness (Figure 9-28).

c. Cavities Causing Numbness
Technique #142: The Tianzong cavity is located in the center of the shoulder blade. It is on the Small Intestine Channel. Striking this cavity (Figure 9-29) can numb the entire shoulder.

Technique #143: It has already been mentioned in Technique #126 that striking the front of the shoulder area can cause the shoulder to go numb (Figure 9-30).

Technique #144: It has already been mentioned in Technique #127 that when the cavity Jianyu on the top of the shoulder is struck (Figure 9-31), the shoulder will become numb.

d. Sealing the Breath (Bih Chi):
Technique #145: Jiuwei or Hsinkan is located in the area of the solar plexus. It is on the Ren Mie. When this cavity is struck with the palm (Figure 9-32), the muscles around the lung will contract and seal the breath.

Technique #146: There are three cavities on the Stomach Channel: Yingchuang, Ruzhong, and Zugen, which are located about one inch

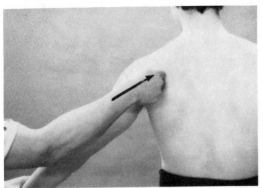

Figure 9-29.

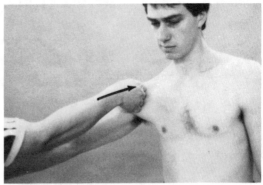

Figure 9-30.

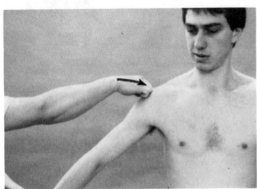

Figure 9-31.

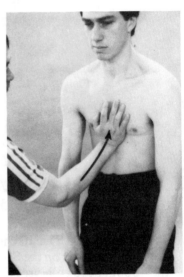

Figure 9-32.

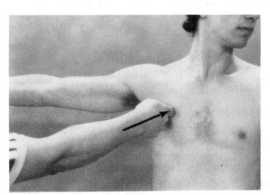

Figure 9-33.

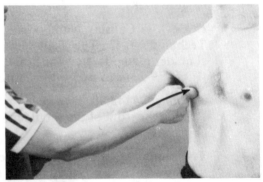

Figure 9-34.

above the nipple, at the nipple, and one inch below the nipple. Striking any of these cavities (Figures 9-33, 9-34, and 9-35) can cause the lung to contract, thus sealing the breath.

Technique #147: The Dabao cavity is located on the side of the chest, on the Spleen Channel. Striking this cavity with either fingers (Figure 9-36) or a knuckle (Figure 9-37) will seal the breath by contracting the lungs.

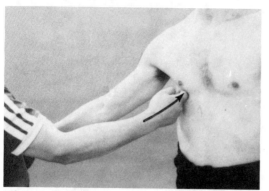

Figure 9-35.

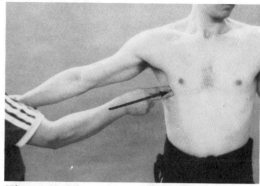

Figure 9-36.

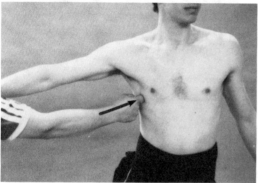

Figure 9-37.

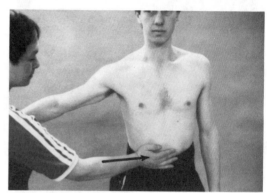

Figure 9-38.

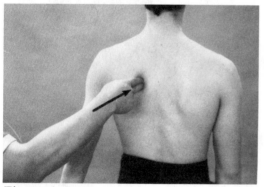

Figure 9-39.

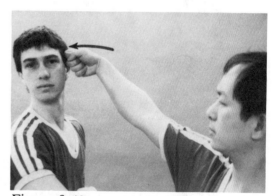

Figure 9-40.

Technique #148: The Tianshu cavity is located on the side of the front of the abdomen, on the Stomach Channel. Striking this cavity (Figure 9-38) can cause the lung muscles to contract and seal the breath.

Technique #149: The Dushu or Zudon cavity is located between the spine and shoulder blade. This cavity is on the Bladder Channel. Striking this cavity (Figure 9-39) can also cause the lungs to contract.

C. Da Shiee Far (Striking the Blood Method) 打血法
Technique #150: The Taiyang (left) and Taiyin (right) cavities are located at the temples on the sides of the head. They are on the Stomach Channel. Striking either of these two cavities with the correct power and method (Figure 9-40) will rupture the artery, causing death.

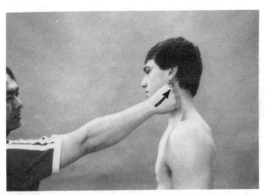

Figure 9-41.

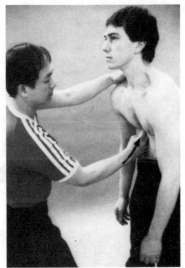

Figure 9-42.

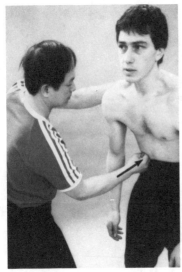

Figure 9-43.

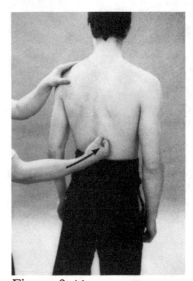

Figure 9-44.

Technique #151: The Yifeng or Ersha cavity is located under the ear. It is on the Sanjiao Channel. Striking this cavity with the right method (Figure 9-41) will rupture the artery.

D. Da Chih Guan (Striking Organs) 打吳官
Technique #152: Striking the solar plexus with the right hand form and power (Figure 9-42) can cause a heart attack.

Technique #153: Striking the right side of the abdomen just under the ribs (Figure 9-43) ruptures the liver.

Technique #154: The kidney is another organ which is weak and easily ruptured when the power penetrates to it (Figure 9-44).

CHAPTER 10

USING CHIN NA

IN A FIGHT

10-1. Introduction

As mentioned earlier, it is much harder to apply most of the grabbing Chin Na techniques to an opponent than to just punch him or use a cavity strike Chin Na. To use a grabbing Chin Na on your opponent is to show him mercy, and to also show him that your fighting ability is much greater than his. Therefore, if you are not confident that you can handle your opponent, you should not take a risk and use grabbing Chin Na. Remember: **TO SHOW MERCY TO YOUR ENEMY MEANS TO BE CRUEL TO YOURSELF.**

When you are in a fight, you should immediately seize your opponent's will, confidence, and fighting spirit. This is spiritual Chin Na. This means that at the beginning of a fight you should use your spirit and confidence to discourage your opponent and make him lose his fighting confidence and spirit. Usually, this spirit and confidence is shown on your face and in the way you look at him. From your eyes and face, your opponent can sense your spirit of vitality, your courage, your confidence, your calmness, and even your Chi capacity and will power. If you can conquer your opponent with this first visual and mental contact, then you have reached the highest level of Chin Na—to seize the opponent's fighting spirit. Remember: **THE HIGHEST FIGHTING ART IS TO FIGHT WITHOUT FIGHTING.**

However, if you are not able to discourage him and you must fight, then you must know a few things. Is your fighting ability greater than his? Will you be able to use grabbing Chin Na to stop the fight? In order to use a grabbing Chin Na successfully, you must first test your opponent and see how his reactions are. This test will reveal his style, and will let you know whether a grabbing Chin Na will work. Remember: **FIGHT SMART AND SAFE, NOT BRAVE AND STUPID.**

In order for your grabbing Chin Na to be effective, your techniques

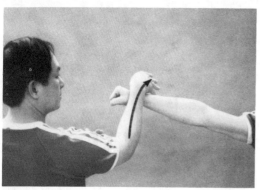

Figure 10-1.

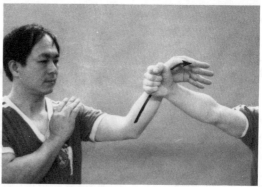

Figure 10-2.

must first of all be fast, natural, and skillful. In a fight, everything happens so fast that you do not have time to think, so your reactions must be natural. You must therefore train so that your reactions are flexible, and you can react quickly and correctly to changing situations. Not only that, you must also know how to fool your opponent and set him up in a position favorable to your Chin Na application. All of these things must be trained constantly until they are part of your natural reaction—only then will you be able to use grabbing Chin Na effectively in a fight.

In addition to the above, there are a number of things you need to train before you can effectively use grabbing Chin Na in a fight. Since you opponent will not cooperate with you, it will be quite different from practicing with a partner. You need to know the ways of setting your opponent up for your Chin Na control. In the next section we will introduce some of the ways of training for this.

10-2. Fundamental Training

All of the following fundamental training will help you learn how to use grabbing Chin Na in a fight. You must practice all of these exercises with many different partners. Once you are familiar with these techniques, you should master them by practicing them with your partners in ways which resemble real fighting.

1. Intercepting and Clamping

The first thing is learning how to intercept a strike. Fights normally start with a punch or a kick. You must know how to intercept an attack and at the same time set your opponent up for your grabbing Chin Na. An important part of this is knowing how to clamp or grab him in a short time. Here we will introduce the common ways of intercepting and clamping in the White Crane style.

Intercept: In White Crane there are two common ways of intercepting, called "Gay" (cover) and "Bo" (repel). Both intercepting techniques imitate the crane's blocking with his wings. When you cover a punch, you use your wrist and hand to cover down the attack from your outside to inside while twisting your body to the side. You may cover his punch from inside (Figure 10-1) or from outside (Figure 10-2). In White Crane, this twisting of the body is called "triangle body"(San Jyue Shen), and is used to avoid exposing your body to attack. This also makes it possible for you to extend your arm further either to attack or to block. Intercepting an attack with cover sets the opponent up so that he has only two options— pulling back or moving downward. If your opponent pulls his attacking

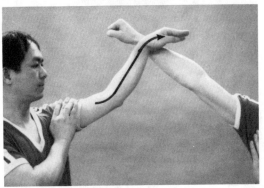

Figure 10-3.

Figure 10-4.

hand back, you should use the opportunity to follow his withdrawal and attack. However, if your opponent does not pull his arm back fast enough, you will have a chance to clamp him and use your grabbing Chin Na. If you opponent tries to move his arm downward, you can easily clamp it if you are prepared. This will be discussed below.

When you repel a punch, you simply use your wrist and hand to repel the punch from inside to outside. You may repel his punch from inside of his arm (Figure 10-3) or from outside (Figure 10-4). As with cover, you have set the opponent up so that he has only two options—pulling back or downward.

If your opponent punches at your lower body, you can also intercept with repel (Figure 10-5). This time you set him up so that he can only withdraw or raise his arm. In either case, you can control him just as you controlled the higher attack.

Clamp: When you intercept an attack, if your opponent does not pull his arm back fast enough you should clamp his punching hand with both hands. This will give you a chance to apply a grabbing Chin Na. Of course, if instead you decide to punch him, simply hit him in an area that was exposed by your interception. When you use cover to intercept, you normally use your other hand to clamp his wrist from underneath (Figures 10-6 and 10-7). When you use repel to intercept, lift your elbow up while your other hand covers down to clamp his hand (Figures 10-8 and 10-9). For an attack to the lower body, simply use the other hand to cover and lock his hand in position (Figure 10-10). In White Crane, this using of both hands to mutually assist each other is called Moo-Tzu Sou (Mother-Son Hand). When mother intercepts, the son will follow to clamp. All White Crane fighting strategies and techniques are generated from this principle.

2. Sticking and Adhering

Normally, when you apply a grabbing Chin Na, your hands do the work. If you are able to stick and adhere to the opponent's limbs with both of your hands, you will not only be able to limit his movements, you will also be able to apply your grabbing Chin Na any time you want. When you stick and adhere, you are able to sense your opponent's intention by your touch. Stick and adhere help you to lead him into your Chin Na trap.

Stick and adhere training have been emphasized in most of the internal martial styles such as Tai Chi Chuan and Hsing Yi, and some of the southern styles such as White Crane, Wing Chun, and Snake. Stick and

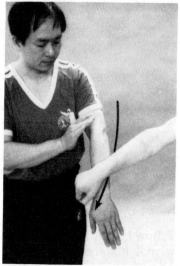

Figure 10-5.

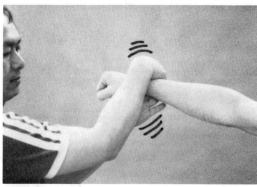

Figure 10-6.

Figure 10-7.

Figure 10-8.

Figure 10-9.

Figure 10-10.

adhere training comes from touching each other's arms and hands, and learning to yield, neutralize, and lead. In order to be able to stick and adhere, you must build up your skin's sensitivity (called skin listening in the internal styles). This sensitivity usually depends on the Chi in your body, and how well you can sense the opponent's Chi. For a detailed discussion, please refer to the author's book: *Advanced Yang Style Tai Chi Chuan, Vol. 1 and Vol. 2.*

3. Wrapping and Coiling

Sticking and adhering are mainly used for defense. Once you have neutralized the opponent's attack, you should also know how to wrap and coil to set up your attack of either striking or grabbing Chin Na. Wrapping is a technique in which your hand wraps around your opponent's hand or arm. It is as if your hand were a piece of flypaper that wraps around and sticks to the opponent so that he cannot get free of it. When you know how to wrap, you will then coil. Coiling enables you to move from one portion of your opponent's arm to another, from one joint to another, so that you can apply your Chin Na control. For a detailed discussion, please refer to the author's advanced Tai Chi Chuan book, Volume 1.

4. Joint Controlling

Joint controlling is called Na Jye. Once you know how to stick and adhere, wrap and coil, then you must know how to control and seal the opponent's joints to limit his movement. Joints allow you to move, and so they are the major target of grabbing Chin Na. If you can control one of the opponent's joints effectively, you will not have any problem in applying any grabbing Chin Na on him. Joint controlling does not mean only grabbing the joint area. The higher level of joint controlling is to stick and adhere instead of grabbing, which is like having a piece of flypaper on your opponent, controlling him and limiting his movements. When you train controlling joints, you also train how to escape from such controlling. For detailed training, refer to the author's advanced Tai Chi Chuan book, Volume 1.

5. Stepping

Stepping is very important in a fight. Correct stepping allows you to position yourself in the most advantageous place for defense or offense. It is just like playing chess. When you occupy the right position, you automatically put your opponent in a passive situation. It is the same in grabbing Chin Na. The right stepping can help you pull the opponent's root easily, can help you to apply a Chin Na technique without putting yourself in danger, and can also help you to use the technique more effectively.

Effective and accurate stepping comes from the accumulated experience of many years of practice. As in playing chess, the more you play, the more tricks you will learn. In a fight, the stepping decides your fighting strategy, and it must happen naturally and automatically since you do not have time to think. Therefore, you should try different ways of stepping with your partners when you practice. Discuss it with your partner, and ponder it by yourself. Remember: **SKILLFUL STEPPING COMES FROM EXPERIENCE.**

6. Sensing (feeling of danger, feeling of controlling) and Reaction

This training comes from mutual practice with a partner. When your partner applies a grabbing Chin Na technique on you, you must use a

Figure 10-11.

Figure 10-12.

counter Chin Na to reverse the situation and try to control him before he has completely controlled you. In the same way, your partner should again use a counter Chin Na against your technique. You and your partner can continue this practice forever since every Chin Na has its counter Chin Na to reverse the situation. You should practice very slowly at first so both of you have time to think of how to react. Then you should increase the speed gradually until you have reached regular fighting speed. This practice will help you to not only master all of the techniques, but also to build up natural reactions for every situation.

10-3. Examples

Application is the accumulation of knowledge and experience. It is impossible to discuss all of the possible applications in such a short chapter. It is your obligation to look for and master the applications after you have learned and practiced from this book. Remember, a master can only teach you the techniques. Whether you will master the techniques and be able to apply them in a practical situation depends on you. When you are in a real situation, nothing is set, and everything depends on your reaction and skill. Here we can only offer you some examples. Hopefully it will lead you in the right direction, and stimulate you to further research and discussion with your partners.

1. Against a Punch:

Technique #155: After you have covered and clamped the opponent's punch from outside of his arm (Figure 10-7), simply circle both your hands (Figure 10-11) and lock his elbow in position (Figure 10-12).

Technique #156: After you have repelled and clamped the opponent's punch from outside of his arm (Figure 10-13), circle your elbow and use it to lock his elbow (Figure 10-14).

Technique #157: After you have repelled and clamped his low punch (Figure 10-15), circle your left arm and control his wrist and elbow (Figure 10-16).

Technique #158: You can also set your opponent up for a Chin Na control offensively. When you punch your opponent with your right

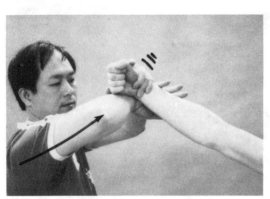

Figure 10-13.

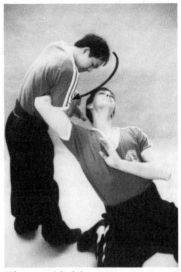

Figure 10-14.

Figure 10-15.

Figure 10-16.

hand, if he intercepts with his right hand (Figure 10-17), use your left hand to grab and control his wrist (Figure 10-18). Immediately use your right hand to control his pinky (Figure 10-19).

Technique #159: This is another example of setting up a Chin Na control through offensive action. When you punch your opponent with your right hand and he intercepts with his left hand (Figure 10-20), use your left hand to grab his left hand (Figure 10-21). Immediately control his wrist with your right hand (Figure 10-22).

2. Against a Kick:
Technique #160: When your opponent kicks you, withdraw your left leg and at the same time use your left arm to intercept and scoop up his leg (Figure 10-23). Lock and control his ankle with your right hand (Figure 10-24). If you desire to attack him, this will give you a chance to kick his groin with your left foot (Figure 10-25).

Technique #161: When your opponent kicks you, scoop up his leg with

Figure 10-17.

Figure 10-18.

Figure 10-19.

Figure 10-20.

Figure 10-21.

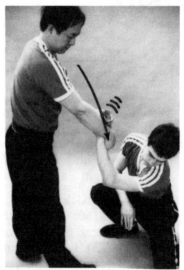

Figure 10-22.

Figure 10-23.

Figure 10-24.

Figure 10-25.

Figure 10-26.

Figure 10-27.

your right hand and use your left hand to lock his ankle (Figure 10-26). Naturally, this will also give you an opportunity to kick his groin (Figure 10-27).

3. Against a Dagger:

Technique #162: When your opponent attacks you with a dagger, holding the point either forward (Figure 10-28) or downward (Figure 10-29), intercept his attack with cover. Then use your other hand to clamp his wrist, and circle the dagger up (Figure 10-30) or to the side (Figure 10-31), or even stab him in the neck (Figure 10-32).

Technique #163: When your opponent attacks you with a dagger, you can also use repel and at the same time use your left hand to lock his elbow (Figure 10-33). Then circle the dagger down to stab him (Figure 10-34).

Figure 10-28.

Figure 10-29.

Figure 10-30.

Figure 10-31.

Figure 10-32.

Figure 10-33.

Figure 10-34.

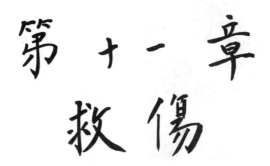

第 十一 章

救傷

CHAPTER 11
TREATMENT OF INJURY

11-1. Introduction

The treatment of injury used to be a required course of study in Chinese martial arts. Injuries occur often, both in combat and in practice. Even in normal daily life, people can be injured during work or other ordinary activities. In ancient times, doctors were not as convenient and accessible as today. It was not until the Sung dynasty (960-1126 A.D.) that any formal training was provided for the realignment of dislocated bones (Jeng Guu Ke), and it was only in the Ming dynasty (1368-1628 A.D.), that official training was given in the setting of broken or fractured bones (Jie Guu Ke). Because the treatment of injury was a necessary aspect of training in Chinese martial arts schools, it has come to be considered a martial artist's duty to use his knowledge to help people and to act as a healer whenever he can. Some martial artists even use this knowledge to provide themselves with extra income when they either grow old or stop training.

The methods of treating injuries are called Dye Da, which means Fall Strike. Dye Da specializes in the treatment of injuries sustained from falling down or getting hit. As a martial artist, you must know how to heal yourself when you are injured. Also, from the standpoint of morality, you must know how to cure your enemy, not just how to injure him.

Even in ancient times, the use of violence was permissible only as a means of self-defense. Once your opponent has surrendered, you have a moral obligation to do all that you can to help him recover. Fighting is a necessary policy only when there is no other solution, and while it is good to win decisively, it is better yet to win decisively without seriously injuring your opponent. By winning in this way you have proven that you could disable or even kill him if necessary. Once you have won the fight, mentally and spiritually you have conquered your enemy's will, and fighting is no longer necessary. Under these circumstances, if you can help your enemy recover from an injury, you may be able to change an enemy into a good friend. Thus, treating your enemy's injuries is not only a moral responsibility, it is a diplomatic and even a strategic tool with which you can accomplish larger goals in life.

Unfortunately, due to the fact that public medical service is so much more available and convenient than it was in ancient times, this kind of training is being ignored more and more over the years. Also, because of the relative ease of treating injuries today, the spirit of injuring the opponent has become stronger than the spirit of forgiving. Martial morality and herbal treatment have become unimportant in today's training.

You however, as a good martial artist, should still gain some knowledge of the curing, emergency treatment, and especially prevention of injury. If you are lacking in this knowledge, you may miss an opportunity to do good, particularly if there are no doctors or hospitals nearby. Furthermore, there are some situations in which immediate action is necessary in order to prevent the injury from becoming worse before a doctor is found. For example, if a joint is dislocated, you can easily put it back by yourself and then have it checked by a doctor. However, if you do nothing and merely take the victim to a hospital, the injured limb will become swollen and the bruises more serious. If you can realign the dislocated joint accurately immediately after the injury occurs, the healing time may be reduced by as much as half.

Before you continue reading this chapter, you should understand that the traditional Chinese method of treatment for some injuries is different from the more familiar Western methods. Take, for example, a jammed finger. The Western method of treatment is to put ice on the injured area in order to prevent further swelling. In ancient times, when ice was not readily found, Chinese martial artists used to massage the injury lightly to loosen the tension in the area. This represents a radical departure from many Western medical ideas. While the Chinese way of thinking is that the massage will help the bruise and Chi to spread out and avoid stagnation, which allows the body's natural healing abilities to more easily and quickly deal with them, the Western way of thinking is that massage will cause the bruise to become worse. The Chinese avoid this by massaging an herb wine called Yaw Shii (herbal wash) or Yaw Jeou (herbal wine) into the injured area. This helps the injury to heal and prevents the bruise and swelling from getting worse. Right after the massage, another herb is used on the injured area in order to convert the Yang (positive) caused by the injury and the massage into Yin (negative), and thereby stop any further swelling. This herb, which is applied directly to the injured area, can be either Yaw Gau (herb ointment), or a Yaw Feen (herb powder) which is mixed with wine or other liquid. The Chinese feel that ice, applied to an injury, will slow down or freeze the circulation of blood and Chi and cause the bruise to become trapped deep in the joint and local cavities, where it may cause arthritis.

It is very difficult to decide which outlook is more correct, especially with the lack of experimentation and empirical evidence in this area. There is theoretical evidence to support both sides, but very little hard proof for either. What is needed is a serious effort on both sides to learn from the other and to design and perform experiments in tandem. According to my past experience, both ways should be used together to generate the most effective results.

Another example of this dichotomy of thought concerns the setting of broken bones. The Chinese way to cure a broken bone is to set the bone, wrap the area with herbs, and then immobilize the limb or area. The patient is instructed to drink certain herb broths (Yaw Tang) right after the bone is set to keep the swelling down, and once the swelling is down to take other herbs either in the form of broth, powder (Yaw Feen), or pill (Yaw Wan) for a week to help the healing. Usually, the healing process is completed in two to three weeks. The Western way involves viewing the break through an x ray during the setting, to insure that the bone is set accurately. The area is then placed in a cast for two to three months. As you can see, the Western way of setting the bone is more accurate than the method used by the traditional Chinese doctors, who relied upon feeling and many years of experience to do the job. However, with the Chinese method the break heals much more quickly than with the Western method.

Both the Chinese and the Western medical treatments have their own advantages and disadvantages. A smart doctor would study both ways and from them find a better way than either one provides alone. This is similar to the way in which Chinese acupuncture and Chi Kung, which used to be considered mysteries, have become more popular in the West, and are now used together with Western medical practices.

Because the author is neither a certified Chinese nor Western doctor of medicine, all that he can offer in this chapter is some of the experiences gathered through the years of instruction provided by his master, and further knowledge gained through his own experimentation. The author hopes that martial artists who are also M.D.'s or qualified Chinese medical practitioners will further this research, so that someday there will be a truly authoritative work on this subject available to the public.

A good Chinese martial artist must know two things about healing. The first of these is diagnosis, the second is treatment. Treatments include: massage, acupuncture, Chi transportation, and herbal treatment. It would be impossible to cover all of the possible injuries in this chapter. Instead, we will discuss some of the more common injuries and hopefully provide you with some knowledge of their prevention and healing. But first, let us discuss diagnosis.

11-2. Diagnosis

Diagnosis is the first and fundamentally most important stage of healing. If your diagnosis is wrong, your treatment may make the patient's condition worse. For example, if the bone is cracked and you think it is just bruised and use massage, you will make the crack worse. If a bone is broken near the joint, but you think it is dislocated and try to put it back, you will make the break worse and cause further pain. Therefore, a correct diagnosis is at least half of the healing process.

Diagnosis usually includes:

1. Looking

a. Skin Color: Skin color can sometimes tell you something. For example, if the skin is blue the injury might be a bruise. The skin color will also tell how wide the bruise has spread. This will give you an idea of how much herb is required to cover the injured area.

b. Appearance: From the appearance of the injury you can roughly tell if the bone is broken or dislocated, or if the swelling is a result of damage to the ligaments or tendons.

2. Asking

a. How: Ask the patient questions about how the injury was sustained and how and where he feels the pain. These questions will usually give you the best idea as to the type and severity of the injury. For example, if he has been struck by a heavy object in the chest, the ribs might be broken and there might be internal bruises.

b. When: When the injury happened is very important. The injury may have occurred a long time ago, but not have bothered the patient until recently. The injury may have just happened only a few hours ago. This information will provide you with an idea as to what kind of herb is required. The herb for an old injury is usually somewhat different from the herb used for a new injury. If a vital cavity has been struck at the right time, you will need to use a special herb to treat the patient or else the patient may die.

c. Where: You must also know exactly where the pain is. Usually, for a deep or an old injury, it is very hard for a doctor to know exactly where the pain is unless the patient tells him.

3. Palpation

a. Feel: Areas which feel painful, hot, swollen, etc. are palpated to determine the nature of the problem. For example, swelling and heat indicates that there is too much Yang in the area. Soft swelling indicates that the Chi is accumulating, while hard swelling indicates a bruise.

b. Press: Press the injured area to see the patient's reaction and test his sensitivity. For example, if pressing causes deep pain in the bone it indicates that the bone may be cracked. If the pain is not deep, it may indicate the presence of a bruise and the accumulation of Chi.

c. Move: Moving the injured area is very important in diagnosis, especially in injuries to the bones and joints. For example, moving the limb gently in different directions will help you to understand how the bone is broken or the joint misplaced. Deep pain in a joint without a misplaced bone indicates an injury to the ligaments and cartilage in the joint.

11-3. Treatment Techniques

The first step in the treatment of any injury is to first diagnose it. If it is simply a bruise, a dislocated joint, or a broken bone, then you would normally first treat the injury as appropriate with your hands, and immediately after cover it with herb. Very often it is also required that the patient take herb internally. There are eight major techniques of hand treatment: Mho (Brush Lightly), Jie (Connect), Duan (Carry Gingerly), Tyi (Raise), Ann (Press), Mo (Rub), Tuei (Push), and Na (Grab). There are also eight minor techniques which are used together with the major techniques. The minor techniques are Lha (Pull), Guah (Suspend), Nhie (Knead), Diing (Support), Song (Send), Ban (Move), Dann (Rebound), and Yau (Shake). These sixteen key hand techniques will enable you to take care of all possible injuries. However, you usually need a teacher to show you the tricks to all of these treatments. Even then, you will still need a lot of experience before you will be able to say that you know how to treat a patient.

In addition to these hand techniques, many martial artists will also more or less know the acupuncture treatments for deep injuries, as well as how to use moxibustion and cupping. Acupuncture involves inserting needles into the Chi cavities to affect the Chi circulation. Moxa is an herb which is burnt to generate a very penetrating heat which is used to cure deep joint problems. Cupping uses cups to suck the Chi or moisture from the pores of the skin to lessen pain.

Furthermore, the martial artist who is serious about learning to treat injuries must also be familiar with herbs. Different herbs have different properties and purposes. One herb might be very poisonous and require another herb to neutralize the poison while still maintaining the beneficial effect. Some herbs might be too Yang and need another Yin herb to neutralize the Yang property. The same herb grown in two different locations will have different levels of effectiveness. The naturally grown, wild herb is usually better than the homegrown herb, and the fresh herb is usually better than the dried herb. Usually, a prescription is a mixture of many different herbs. You must know the purposes and properties of every herb. Then you will know how to mix them without producing side-effects in your patients. In addition, you must also learn how to make herbal ointments. For example, too much heat will make them too positive. All of this knowledge takes more than ten years to learn and master under the instruction of a qualified Chinese master or doctor. Since all of this knowledge has to be passed down by a qualified herbal master, we will not discuss it in very great detail. However, we will list some of the common prescriptions for general purposes in Appendix B. You should be able to purchase these herbs in Taiwan, Japan, Hong Kong, Beijing, or any other oriental city. In this section we will only discuss some of the hand techniques.

1. Mho (Touch Lightly): Mho means to feel or touch lightly with the fingers, to caress, to stroke. Mho is the first technique in massage. Brushing the skin lightly around and over the injured area can make it relax, loosening the tense muscles. This allows the Chi and blood to circulate freely again. Also, this sensitive touching helps you to understand the injury through your feeling. Sometimes Chi Kung experts can remove the excess Chi at the injured area by touching, which helps the healing.

2. Jie (Connect): Jie means to connect, to put together, and refers to the setting of broken bones. Jie in Dye Da requires a lot of experience. If you do not use the correct amount of power, you will not be able to pull the broken bones apart and then gently put them into the right position.

3. Duan (Carry Gingerly): Duan means to lift or carry gingerly. Duan is also a way of connecting. When you move the broken bones together, you have to be very careful. Duan in Chinese also means holding, like holding a plate in your hands. Duan is also used to relocate misplaced bones and joints.

4. Tyi (Raise): Tyi means to raise, to lift, or to move up. It is also a method for either connecting broken bones or relocating joints.

5. Ann (Press): Ann means to press down. Ann and Mo (rub) are generally used together and are called massage. Massage is used to remove the excess Chi and bruises which collect and stagnate in injured areas.

6. Mo (Rub): Mo means to chafe, to scour, to rub, to feel with the hand, and to massage. Mo is commonly used together with Ann (press). The purpose of press and rub is to get rid of the excess Chi and bruises.

7. Tuei (Push): Tuei means to push. This technique is mainly used for relocating or setting broken bones. When the bone is broken in several places, very often you will have to push the pieces together in order to set them correctly. When a rib is broken, pushing is also necessary to put the bone back into its original position.

8. Na (Grab): Na means to grab or to hold. Na is used to hold the patient's limb steady so that the connection process can be performed. Na is also used when one person holds the patient's limb while another person relocates or connects the joint or bone.

9. Lha (Pull): Lha is a major technique in the connecting and relocation of a damaged bone or joint. When a bone is broken or the joint dislocated, the extreme pain causes the muscles to contract. Before you can relocate or set the bone you must first pull the bones apart.

10. Guah (Suspend): Guah means to suspend or to hang up. Guah is a technique for relocating or connecting joints and bones. It is commonly used in relocating the shoulder joint.

11. Nhie (Knead): Nhie means to knead, to pinch, or to squeeze and press with the fingers. Nhie is a technique of massage. Nhie is commonly used with Dann (rebound). When Nhie is used on the limbs, you use fingers to pinch or grab a muscle, and shake or rebound it. When Nhie is used at the joint it is used to pinch the tendons. Nhie is also commonly used for diagnosis and to test the reactions of the patient.

12. Diing (Support): Diing means to support or to push up. Diing is also a technique used for dislocated joints and broken bones.

13. Song (Send): Song is mainly used for dislocated and broken bones. When the joint is misplaced or the bone is broken, you must first pull the bones apart, and then direct and lead the bones back to their original position as the contracting muscles pull them back together.

14. Ban (Move): Ban means to move. Sometimes the bones are broken into pieces, and you must move the pieces back into their correct alignment. For example, the kneecap can be moved away from the knee when injured, and so you must move it back. Sometimes, after you have made the connection, you move the limb or joint to a different angle to see if you have placed the bone back correctly.

15. Dann (Rebound): Dann means to rebound or to spring. It is used in massage. You grab the tendon and pull it up, and then let it go. This reduces muscle tension and readjusts any jamming. Usually, if you do this right after the jam, you can reduce the severity of the injury by half.

16. Yau (Shake): Yau means to shake. Yau is another techniques used in massage. You simply hold the muscle and shake it. This reduces muscle tension and lets the muscle relax.

The above techniques are the most common hand treatments. There are many other methods of hand treatment which are not listed here. Which techniques you actually use depends both upon the situation and upon which master you studied with. In similar situations, one master may use one method while another may use a different method. Practice treating minor injuries first, and gradually you will gain the experience and know-how to treat larger, more serious ones.

11-4. Treatment of Common Injuries
Most of the common injuries causes by Chin Na occur in the joint areas. The injury can be deep—in the ligament and cartilage, for instance, or shallow—as in surface bruises. They can also be as serious as a broken bone, or as slight as an overstimulated tendon. We will first discuss the treatment of joint injuries and follow up with a discussion of injuries which do not occur in the joint area.

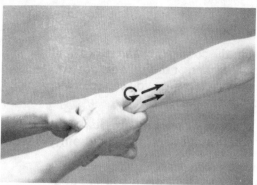

Figure 11-1.

Joint Injuries:

Before we discuss joint injuries, you should first understand one thing. When the joint is hurt because of twisting and bending, extreme pain will result. The pain will cause the muscles to tense up and contract, which in turn causes the Chi to accumulate and stagnate in the injured area. If you can pull the muscles immediately after they are injured, you will extend and stretch the muscles and prevent them from contracting, thus preventing this accumulation and helping the Chi to flow. This will decrease the seriousness of the injury. For example, if you have hurt your wrist, you should immediately pull every finger first, and then lightly massage the wrist. This will ease the muscle tension, which usually reduces the swelling and keeps stiffness from developing the next day. At the same time it spreads out the bruise so that the body's natural healing abilities can more easily deal with it. When you massage, use circular motions, and then push either up or down (Figure 11-1). If the joint is misplaced or the bone is broken, naturally, you should not use the same technique as you would in treating a jammed finger or shoulder. Here, we will discuss the common joint injuries:

1. Muscle and Tendon Injury:

Muscle and tendon injuries are the most common injuries to the joint areas. Muscle injury is generally caused when the muscle is overstretched or is twisted to the wrong angle, causing the muscle fiber to tear. When the tendons and muscles are injured at the joint area there is immediate pain, which usually makes the muscles and tendons contract. This contraction and pain will cause bruises, Chi accumulation, and swelling.

Your first reaction when you have injured a joint area, if it is not a broken or misplaced bone, should be to pull and stretch the injured muscles, following up with a light massage and the application of herb wine to the injured area. For example, if the wrist is injured, pull every finger, both individually and together. This will relax the muscles and tendons, easing the pain and preventing the bruises and Chi accumulation from getting more serious. Right after this, if ice is available, place ice on the injured area. This will significantly help the swelling go down.

About half an hour later, check the injury. If the damage is serious, be sure there are no broken bones or dislocated joints before you massage any further or apply herb wine. When you massage, be careful to use only enough power to produce a slight pain—caused by the stimulation—but not serious pain. If massage causes too much pain it will agitate the area and make the swelling worse. Right after you massage, dress it with the herb ointment or herb powder mixed with alcohol, wrap it and leave it overnight. Remember **IF THE SKIN IS BROKEN IN THE INJURED AREA, DO NOT PLACE THE HERB ON IT**. Some of the herbs are poisonous if they come in contact with the blood.

The next morning, if the swelling is still serious, repeat the process of massage and dressing. Sometimes the herb will irritate the skin and cause itching. If this happens, stop the herb application to the skin, wash it clean, and apply some soothing ointment to the area.

2. Ligament and Cartilage Injury:

Ligament and cartilage injury is usually caused when the joint is twisted to the wrong angle, or when it is twisted and bent, causing the tissue to tear or the ligament to become disconnected from the bone. This causes extreme pain, bruises, and stagnant Chi flow. If the bruise is not eliminated, the Chi will become trapped deep in the joint, causing swelling of the periosteum (the membrane around the bone). This torn tissue and deep joint inflammation is usually difficult to heal through massage. The common cure is to use acupuncture, cupping, and external herb treatment. Ligament and cartilage damage is accompanied by tendon damage. The tendons, which protect against an outside twisting attack, are the joint's first line of defense. When the tendons fail to protect the joint, the ligament has to absorb some of the attack, although it is weak and poorly designed for this. Therefore, when the joint is injured you should go about healing it through the use of massage and the application of herb. After the swelling has gone down, you will be able to see if the ligament is also damaged.

Very often an injury to a joint area will heal by itself over a period of time. This is because the joint is exercised as you go about your daily activities, which allows the accumulated Chi and blood to dissipate. However, you must understand that a deep bruise in the joint can remain for a long time, causing inflammation of the ligament and the periosteum, and later in life you may develop arthritis. Do not ignore deep pain. In many cases, the practice of Chi Kung can heal arthritis and deep bruises.

3. Misplaced Bones:

When a joint is bent beyond the point to which the ligament can stretch, the ligament may become disconnected from the bones it links and the bones will be misplaced. This may be either a slight separation or a full dislocation where the bone comes completely out of its socket. This is a serious injury and can cause severe damage. Once the joint is misplaced in this manner, the damage becomes permanent and the joint can easily be misplaced thereafter. When the joint is dislocated, the first thing to do is to relocate it before the bruise and Chi accumulation get any worse. If you wait too long, the pain will cause the muscles to contract, causing severe Chi stagnation. After you have placed the bones back in their correct position, you should then apply the herb around the joint area to help it heal. The internal herb is also helpful, although harder to find outside of the Orient. If massage is necessary, do not agitate the joint. Massage gently and keep away from the joint area.

There are many ways of placing the bone back together after it has been misplaced. Here we will only give you some examples. The general trick is to pull and bend. When you pull, pull the bones apart slightly and then push them into the connecting position. Later, bend the joint and place it in. Do not over-pull the joint, it will make the damage more serious. However, if you do not pull it apart enough, the joint will not be set correctly.

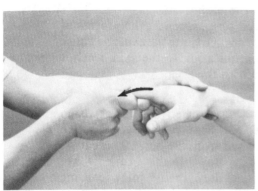

Figure 11-2.

Figure 11-3.

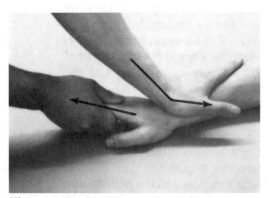

Figure 11-4.

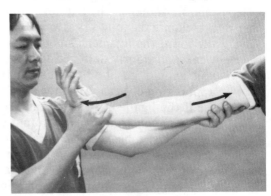

Figure 11-5.

Example 1: Misplaced finger joint. When a finger joint is misplaced, simply pull it out gently (Figure 11-2) and bend it (Figure 11-3) to move the bone back into the correct position.

Example 2: Misplaced wrist. The wrist is composed of eight bones. Sometimes, one of the bones is misplaced, causing a big bump on the surface of the wrist. When this happens, simply pull the fingers out steadily to expand the wrist joint as you push the dislocated bone back (Figure 11-4).

Example 3: Misplaced elbow. When the elbow is misplaced, pull the forearm with one hand while holding the upper arm steady with the other hand (Figure 11-5). Line up the forearm and upper arm and then bend (Figure 11-6).

Example 4: Misplaced shoulder. Since the shoulder is stronger, you will usually need another person to help you hold the patient steady. Ask the third person to hold the patient's chest tightly and steadily while you pull the patient's arm (Figure 11-7). Then bend his arm toward his body and place it back (Figure 11-8).

4. Broken or Chipped Bone at the Joint:

Broken bones at the joint are a very serious matter. Very often the

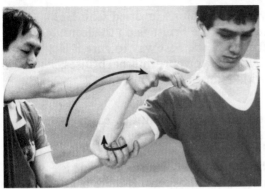

Figure 11-6.

Figure 11-7.

Figure 11-8.

broken bone is only a tiny shard and will not be sensed by a doctor. Also, it is very often the case that there is more than one shard of bone present. When this happens, the best way to deal with it is to take the patient to the hospital and have it examined under an x ray machine. After the connection, place the herb on the surface of the skin over the injury and take the other herb internally (if it is available).

Non-Joint Injuries:
1. Bruises:
  General Bruises: General bruises can be caused when any part of the body is agitated; for example, when it is hit by a hard object. To treat this kind of bruise, put ice on it as soon as possible, if it is readily available. This will prevent the bruise from becoming more serious. About half an hour later, you should begin massaging the area to spread out the bruise. Once the bruise is spread out, the body will be better able to heal it by itself, and you should leave it alone. Normally, when you massage you should use the herb wine. If you do not have herb wine, alcohol, ginger root, or even warm water will help the bruise to spread out. After the massage, you will not usually need to use any herb ointment or herb powder on the bruise, unless it is very serious.

  Internal Bruises: An internal bruise is usually caused by a hit from a heavy object to the chest, a penetrating Jing strike, or a joint control Chin Na. Normally, if the bruise is deep inside of the body, such as on the inside of the rib, massage will not help to spread the bruise. You will then have to rely on herb applied to the surface of the injured area as well as the herb which is taken internally to eliminate the bruise. According to some recent reports, eating raw or partially cooked onions or dried Chinese radish will often eliminate internal bruises. If the bruise is on the joint, such as those caused by Chin Na control, then the best way to cure it is through the use of acupuncture. It is crucial that you cure internal bruises, for if you do not they may cause arthritis later in life.

2. Broken and Cracked Bones:

Broken Bones: Generally, a broken bone can be identified easily as such unless it is a small bone which is broken or a bone which is only chipped. This is especially true in the joint areas. It is difficult to tell if a bone is only cracked, and an x ray is the only way to be sure. If a bone is broken, the first choice is to take the person to a hospital. If there is no professional care available, set it immediately before swelling and bruises develop. Splint the limb, and then take the victim to a hospital as soon as possible to check the connection under an x ray. If you are able to use Chinese herbal treatments, you may be able to shorten the healing time to 2-3 weeks.

Cracked Bones: If deep pain is felt when the injured area is pressed, do not massage it. First have it checked out under an x ray. It might be a cracked bone. If this is the case, massage will make it worse. Simply put the herb on it and immobilize the bone until it is healed.

3. Ruptured Artery:

A ruptured artery caused by an attack to a vital area such as the femoral artery at the temple is usually fatal. No emergency treatment is possible. The only chance is to get the victim to a hospital immediately.

4. Ruptured Capillary:

Very often when part of the body is hit by a hard object, especially in the wrist area, you will see a bump appear suddenly. When you touch it, it will not feel hard. This is most likely a ruptured capillary. When this happens, simply use your finger to press down on the injured area and hold it there for about five minutes (Figure 11-9). Remember, do not massage it, simply press it down and it will be all right.

5. Ruptured or Shocked Organs:

The liver and the kidney are the most frequently ruptured organs, and it is usually fatal. If the victim is rushed to the hospital, Western medicine might be able to save him. The organ that is shocked most frequently is the heart. The correct kind of strike can cause a heart attack, which is usually fatal. However, if the correct modern revival techniques are used, the victim's life may be saved.

6. Sealed Vein/Artery in the Neck:

When the vein/artery is sealed in the neck, it will not cause death immediately. If you can revive the patient within five minutes, he will recover without too much brain damage. If a patient remains unconscious for more than a few minutes after the vein/artery is sealed, his brain will die from oxygen starvation. To revive a victim of this technique, you must push the space between the sixth and seventh thoracic vertebrae with your palm (Figure 11-10). When the power is right, it will reopen the seal by contracting the muscles in the back of the neck. **WE STRONGLY URGE YOU NOT TO USE SEALING THE VEIN/ARTERY TECHNIQUES UNLESS ABSOLUTELY NECESSARY, BECAUSE THERE IS A VERY GREAT DANGER YOU MAY UNINTENTIONALLY KILL THE PERSON.**

Figure 11-9.

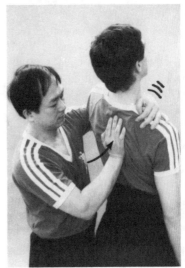

Figure 11-10.

7. Sealed Breath:

When the breath is sealed, it is usually not as dangerous as when the vein/artery is sealed. The patient is temporarily short of breath. If he passes out, use water to wipe his face and forehead, and massage his chest to help him recover. If only one side of the lung is sealed, you can decrease the pressure on it by pushing on the other side (Figure 11-11). This causes the muscles on that side to tense up, and thereby relaxes the other side. The push should not be too hard.

8. Groin Attack:

A kick to the groin is extremely painful, and is sometimes even fatal. This is because the Chi channel which passes through the groin also passes through the liver. When pain is generated in the groin, the shock can pass to the liver and possibly cause death. When someone is hit in the groin, immediately lift the patient on your back with his face upward and shake up and down (Figure 11-12). This will stretch the contracted muscles in the groin area and quickly reduce the pain. Occasionally you may find that one or even both testicles have been pushed up into the abdomen. To correct this, simply have the patient squat down and use both hands to gently press down on the front of the abdomen (Figure 11-13).

9. Stagnant Chi:

Stagnant or blocked Chi is usually caused by a strike to a cavity area. The strike causes bruising or swelling in the cavity area, which blocks the Chi channel. This will cause serious problems if the blockage is not removed and the channel reopened. General treatment for blocked Chi in a shallow cavity should begin with massage, followed by the application of herb to the surface of the skin over the cavity, and the administration of the internally taken herb. For deeper blockages, acupuncture is necessary, along with the administration of the internally taken herb.

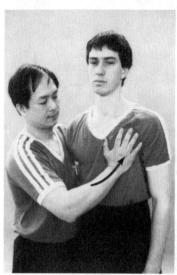

Figure 11-11.   Figure 11-12.   Figure 11-13.

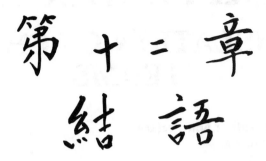

CHAPTER 12
CONCLUSION

With more than five thousand years of research and training behind them, the Chinese martial arts cover a very broad range of techniques. They use the hands, the legs, and numerous weapons. They encompass the external and the internal, the physical and the mental. Chin Na is only a tiny portion of the total training. As mentioned in the first chapter, all we can show you in this book are those techniques which can be seen physically. The higher levels of Chin Na, which require the development of Chi and Jing, must be felt, and usually they can only be learned through oral instruction from a qualified teacher. If you wish to reach the highest level of skill, but cannot find an instructor, then you must read, attend seminars, ponder, and practice. If you persevere, then after several years of training you may find yourself at the doorway to the higher, internal side of the art.

Although we have not presented all of the possible Chin Na techniques, we have given you the root of Chin Na. If you build wisely on this root, you should be able to grow and bloom. If you just learn the techniques by rote, and never learn to develop yourself through your own research, then you should not be called a master of Chin Na. A master must know how to keep the old and develop the new, while always following the correct principles and rules. I hope in the future to see more publications by other instructors, presenting better and more advanced techniques, as well as techniques from other styles of martial arts.

APPENDIX A
TRANSLATION OF CHINESE TERMS

About the Author and Preface

少林擒拿 Shaolin Chin Na
金紹敏 Gin Shao-Fon
揚俊敏 Yang, Jwing-Ming
武術 Wushu
功夫 Kung Fu
白鶴 Pai Huo
曾金灶 Cheng Gin-Gsao
太極拳 Tai Chi Chuan
高濤 Kao Tao
淡江學院 Tamkang College
台北縣 Taipei Hsien
長拳 Chang Chuan
李茂清 Li Mao-Ching
國術 Kuoshu
勁 Jing
洗髓氣功 Shii Soei Chi Kung
連步拳 Lien Bu Chuan
功力拳 Gung Li Chuan
一路埋伏 Yi Lu Mei Fu
嘯虎燕 Shaw Fu Ien
十字趟 Shih Tzu Tan
分筋 Fen Gin
錯骨 Tsuoh Guu
閉氣 Bih Chi
斷脉 Duann Mie
抓筋 Jua Gin
點穴 Tien Hsueh
點脉 Dim Mak

Chapter 1

擒凶 Chin Shiong
六合八法 Liu Ho Ba Fa
意 Yi
清朝 Ching dynasty
釵 Sai
空氣 Korn Chi
氣脉 Chi Mie
血脉 Shiee Mie
督脉 Du Mie
任脉 Ren Mie
子午流注 Tzu Wuu Lieu Ju

Chapter 2

小圈 Shao Jiuan
中圈 Jong Jiuan

大圈 Da Jiuan
神 Shen
鶴爪抓 Huo Jao Jua
飛翅 Fei Chyh
指波 Jyy Bo
達摩 Da Mo
易筋經 Yi Gin Ching
外丹 Wai Dan
石鎖 Shyr Suoo
竹把 Jwu Ba

Chapter 3

握指翻 Woh Jyy Fan
單指握 Dan Jyy Woh
多指握 Duo Jyy Woh
反背轉 Faan Bei Joan
節壓法 Gieh Ya Far
姆指壓 Moo Jyy Ya
下壓指 Shiah Ya Jyy
上刁法 Shang Diau Far
小指扣 Shao Jyy Kow
上分指 Shang Fan Jyy
轉手法 Joan Sou Far
轉分指 Joan Fen Jyy
扣轉節 Kow Joan Gieh
小指板 Shao Jyy Ban
分叉法 Fen Cha Far
上刁分 Shang Diau Fen
下刁分 Shiah Diau Fen
小纏指 Shao Charn Jyy
双分指 Shuang Fen Jyy
緊鎖法 Jin Shou Far
扣龍頭 Kow Long Tao
扣龍尾 Kow Long Wei
上刁指 Shang Diau Jyy

Chapter 4

纏法 Charn Far
小纏手一1 Shao Charn Sou-1
小纏手一2 Shao Charn Sou-2
大纏手 Da Charn Sou
反纏手 Faan Charn Sou
壓腕 Ya Wan
前壓腕 Chyan Ya Wan
上壓腕 Shang Ya Wan
下內壓腕 Shiah Ney Ya Wan

溝宗	Suigao
天宗	Tianzong
鳩尾	Jiuwei
心坎	Hsinkan
乳中	Ruzhong
膺窗	Yingchuang
乳根	Zugen
大包	Dabao
天樞	Tianshu
督俞	Dushu
入洞	Zudon
太陽	Taiyang
太陰	Taiyin
翳風	Yifeng
耳下	Ersha

Chapter 10

盖	Gay
撥	Bo
三角身	San Jyue Shen
拿節	Na Jye

Chapter 11

宋朝	Sung dynasty
正骨科	Jeng Guu Ke
明朝	Ming Dynasty
接骨科	Jie Guu Ke
跌打	Dye Da
藥洗	Yaw Shii
藥酒	Yaw Jeou
藥膏	Yaw Gau
藥湯	Yaw Tang
藥粉	Yaw Feen
藥丸	Yaw Wan
摸	Mho
接	Jie
端	Duan
提	Tyi
按	Ann
摩	Mo
推	Tui
拿	Na
拉	Lha
掛	Guah
捏	Nhie
頂	Diing
送	Song
搬	Ban
彈	Dann
搖	Yaw

Chapter 12

APPENDIX A

APPENDIX B

大生地	Da Sheng Di

APPENDIX B
PRESCRIPTIONS OF CHINESE HERBS

Every traditional Chinese martial style has many herbal prescriptions. Traditionally, they have been kept secret from other styles. There is no doubt that the herbs used by one style can be quite different from the herbs used by another style, since there are hundreds of herbs which can serve the same purpose. Listed here are only a few prescriptions. An interested reader can easily collect most of the prescriptions in bookstores in Taiwan, since they are no longer considered secret. In this appendix we will introduce some prescriptions for herb wine, herb powder for general injury, broken bone external use, broken bone internal use, and herbs for internal injury.

A. YAW SHII (Herb Wash) OR EXTERNAL YAW JEOU (External Herb Wine)

Most of the external herb wines cannot be drunk because toxic herbs are used. The following prescriptions can be purchased pre-mixed. Simply place the herb in a jar and pour in hard liquor or pure alcohol (though pure alcohol tends to evaporate very fast). Chinese people commonly use rice wine because it is inexpensive and easily available in China. Sweet wines do not work out as well. The top of the liquid should be at least one or two inches higher than the top of the herb, because the dried herbs will absorb some of the liquid. Then you should seal the jar completely. Glass is the best material for the container, because it will not react with the contents. Keep the herb in a dark place for at least 40 days. The longer the herb is in the liquid, the stronger the herb wine is. The more liquid you use, the weaker the herb wine will be.

When you wish to use the herb wine, pour what you need into a bowl or other container. If you do not finish what you have poured out, **DO NOT PUT IT BACK INTO THE JAR. THIS WILL CONTAMINATE THE CLEAN HERB WINE.** Also, do not use the herb wine on an open wound, because it may enter your body and cause problems. In China, ten U.S. dollars should buy you one of these prescriptions, which should last you for years. All three of these prescriptions are used to get rid of bruises and to prevent swelling during massage. They can be prepared as described above.

B. External Yaw Feen for Common Injuries (Herb Powder)

External Yaw Feen is usually used to cover the injured area to reduce swelling and help healing after massage. It cannot be eaten. If your skin is broken, do not use the herb. It might get into your body through the wound and generate side effects. When you order it, it should come in powder form, since this is indicated in the prescription. Once you have received the herb powder, seal it in a jar and do not open it unless you need it.

When you use the herb powder, pour out enough herb to cover the injured area. Mix the herb with wine or herb wine so that it has the

A. YAW SHII (Herb Wash) OR EXTERNAL YAW JEOU (External Herb Wine)

洗藥方（1）

柳枝三錢　小茴香三錢　細辛三錢　白芷三錢　當歸尾三錢　桂枝三錢　紅花三錢　赤芍三錢　茯苓三錢　川芎三錢　澤蘭三錢　北芥三錢　乙金三錢　金銀花三錢　甘草三錢　防風三錢　獨活三錢　羌活三錢

酒二斤浸四天方可用

洗藥方（2）

細辛三錢　茯苓三錢　川芎三錢　當歸尾三錢　桃仁三錢　沒藥三錢　乙金三錢　北芥三錢　澤蘭三錢　紅花三錢　甘草三錢

酒二斤浸四天方可用

洗藥方（3）

血竭三錢　當歸三錢　川芎三錢　北芥三錢　沉香三錢　白芷三錢　當歸三錢　桂枝三錢　紅花三錢　細辛三錢

酒二斤浸四天方可用

consistency of putty. Cover the injured area with the mixture, cover the mixture with a sheet of plastic, and bind it up. After 24 hours unwrap it and wash it clean with warm water. If the swelling is still serious, massage the area and apply another dose of herb. Sometimes the herb will irritate your skin, causing it to itch. If this happens, stop using the herb. Simply wash the injured area clean and apply a soothing ointment. After a few days try the herb again. There are three prescriptions introduced here. In the second prescription you will find a package of black-colored herb called Da Sheng Di. This herb is negative and helps the swelling to go

（1）甲粉方一

（2）乙粉方二

（3）甲粉方三

down very fast. When you use the herb, first place the Da Sheng Di in a bowl and cover it with wine. Wait for two hours until the herb becomes soft. Mash it to a uniform consistency and mix it with the herb powder, and then mix with wine as described above.

C. Misplaced or Broken Bones

The following prescriptions are used specifically for bone treatment. Normally, for broken bones, you apply herb to the surface of the injury, and also take the internal prescriptions to keep the swelling down and speed up the healing. We will introduce two prescriptions for external application, two for internal use to keep the swelling down, and finally two for helping the healing.

1. External Usage:

The preparation is the same as in Section B. The only difference in

(2)

楠查三錢　丁香五分

桃仁　乳香五分　桂枝三錢

木香　没药五分　赤芍五錢

續斷　归尾三錢　白芍五錢

骨碎補　生地　桂枝　川芎

以上共研細末外敷方

(1)

丁香五分　乳香以火炮

桃仁　没药五分　桂枝三錢

木香五錢　归尾三錢

桂枝　川芎　赤芍

骨碎補　生地黄　山甲五分

研細末外敷

treatment is that after you have wrapped up the injury you must immobilize it so that the broken bone does not separate again.

2. Internal Usage to Keep the Swelling Down:

We are introducing two prescriptions for this purpose. To prepare these herbs, add one and a half cups of water and cook it over medium heat until only 80% of the water remains. Drink the liquid. The herb can be used one more time, but then it must be discarded. Usually you will need at least three to five packages of herb (six to ten doses) to bring the swelling completely down, and then you can switch to the herbs in the next section which will speed the healing.

3. Internal Usage to Help Healing:

The following two prescriptions are to help the broken bone reconnect in a short time. To prepare the first prescription, add about one and a half cups of wine or liquor and cook over medium heat for about half an hour, then drink the broth. The herb can be used again. Chinese people will often cook the herb with chicken for an hour, and then drink the broth and eat the chicken. When chicken is used, cook it with the bones.

Prepare the second prescription the same way, except use half water and half wine.

D. Internal Usage for Internal Bruises

The following prescriptions are taken internally to get rid of internal bruises. Once you purchase the herb powder, seal it in a jar until you need

（一）接骨退癀方一

生地　當歸尾　澤蘭　天花　桂枝　烏藥
乳香　柳枝　續斷

水碗半煎八分服

（二）接骨退癀方二

續斷　柳枝　大黃　乳香　桔梗　甘草

水碗半煎八分服

（一）接骨補骨方

生地　酒烏藥　澤蘭　當歸　川芎　乳香　骨碎補　汗
續　北　密　油桂　川七　伏苓　酒川　蒼

酒煎服

（二）接骨食方

桂枝　川七　大茴　歸中　生地　五加皮　赤芍　汗
沒藥　丁香　骨碎補　甘草　桔梗　羌活　乳香

水酒各碗半煎八分服

it. Very often the same herbs are ordered in non-powdered form so that they can be cooked with water or wine for serious internal injury. Also, the herb can also be placed in liquor and stored away for emergency use. When an emergency arises, drink the liquid, or else cook the herb and wine with chicken. Many powdered forms of internal herb cannot be taken in large amounts, because they are too strong and therefore dangerous to your health. To use the powdered herb prescriptions, take one teaspoonful in the morning and one in the evening.

INDEX

SELECTED BOOKS FROM YMAA

SELECTED VIDEOTAPES FROM YMAA

DVDS FROM YMAA

POSTERS FROM YMAA

more products available from...

YMAA Publication Center, Inc. 楊氏東方文化出版中心

4354 Washington Street Roslindale, MA 02131
1-800-669-8892 • ymaa@aol.com • www.ymaa.com